Christian Liberty Nature Reader

Book Two

Written by
Julia McNair Wright

Revised and Edited by
Edward J. Shewan

Christian Liberty Press

Arlington Heights, Illinois

ORIGINAL TITLE: Sea-Side And Way-Side No. 1, by Julia McNair Wright
ORIGINAL PUBLISHER: D.C. Health; © 1891, 1901

2010 Printing

General editorship by Michael J. McHugh
Revised and edited by Edward J. Shewan
Copyediting by Diane C. Olson and Belit M. Shewan
Cover design by Eric D. Bristley
Layout and graphics by Edward J. Shewan

A publication of

Christian Liberty Press
502 West Euclid Avenue
Arlington Heights, IL 60004
www.christianlibertypress.com

ISBN 978-1-930092-52-5
1-930092-52-0

Set in Berkeley
Printed in the United States of America

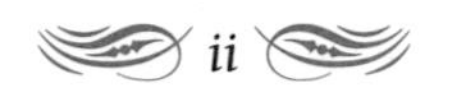

CONTENTS

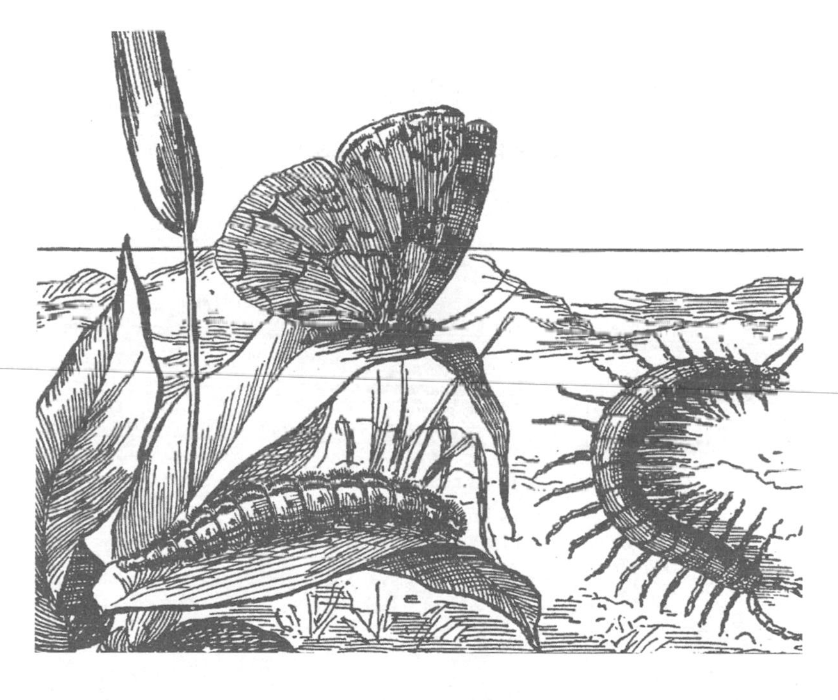

Fantasy

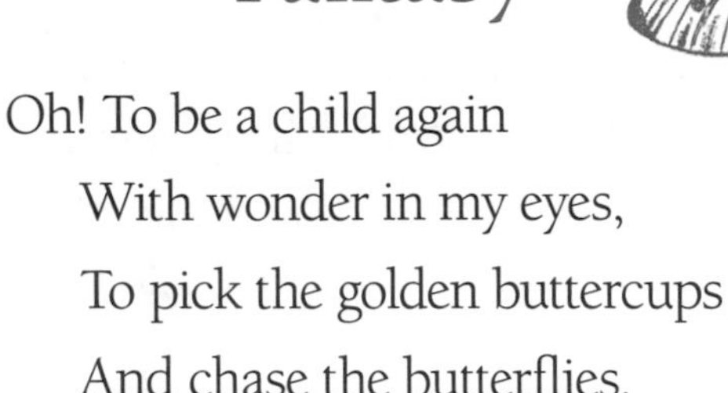

Oh! To be a child again
With wonder in my eyes,
To pick the golden buttercups
And chase the butterflies.

Oh! To be a child again
Climbing a gently sloping hill,
To watch the world awaken
And hear the whippoorwill.

Oh! To be a child again
Running in the sun-warm breeze,
To kiss alive the blossoms
And watch unfolding leaves.

Nora Norton

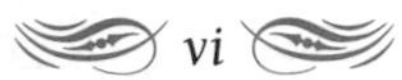

Preface

We are honored to bring you a classic textbook. This particular textbook is designed to not only improve a student's reading skills and comprehension, but to also increase the student's understanding of and interest in God's wonderful creation.

To be able to read is to have the foundation for all subsequent education. The child whose reading training is deficient grows up to become the child who is frustrated, in despair, and soon to join the ranks of the drop-outs, the pushed-outs, the unemployed and the unemployable.

Millions of Americans are handicapped in their reading skills. The "look-say" method of teaching, rather than the older "phonics" technique, has resulted in a generation of functional illiterates. It has been revealed that the U.S. literacy rate has dropped to the level of Burma and Albania and is rapidly approaching that of Zambia.

Not only is the method of teaching reading of vital importance, but also the literary quality of the reading material. So much of what passes for "modern" readers in education today is nothing more than pablum that stresses "social adjustment."

The Bible says we are to do "all for the glory of God" (I Corinthians 10:31). Reading for God's glory necessitates reading material that draws attention to Him

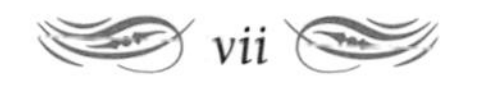

and His truth, that reflects His majesty, and that meets the standards of the Holy Scriptures. What this means is that we should take any reading selection to Philippians 4:8 and ask these simple questions: "Is it true? Is it noble? Is it right? Is it pure? Is it lovely? Is it admirable? Is it excellent? Is it praiseworthy?"

As we look at the American readers of days gone by, we find that the biblical standard was followed. Such readers featured the finest British and American authors who emphasized God, morality, the wonders of creation, and respect for one's country.

The *Christian Liberty Nature Reader* series follows the pattern of the past. Believing that the student can gain an enhanced appreciation for God by studying His creation (Psalm 19:1; Romans 1:20), this textbook seeks to present the majestic splendor of His handiwork.

It is our prayer that this series will give to the reader the joy that is to be associated with "good reading," and that the knowledge imparted will help "make wise the simple" (Psalm 19:7).

Dr. Paul D. Lindstrom

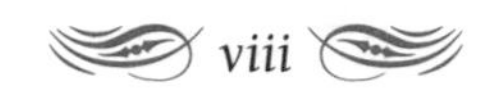

Chapter One
All About Crabs

Mr. and Mrs. Crab

This is a picture of Mr. and Mrs. Crab. Do you see the round hole? It is the door of their house. Mr. Crab lives in the sand by the sea. He has a smooth, flat outer "shell" on his back, eight legs, and two "hands," or **claws**. One claw is large; the other claw is small. Mr. Crab fights with the big claw and takes his food with the little one or with both claws.

Mr. Crab digs out his house in the sand; he makes a place for a hall, a bedroom, and a **pantry**. Mrs. Crab does not dig.

Both her hands are small and weak. She gets food to put into the pantry, and she never fights. If she is in any trouble, she runs home or to a hole in a rock.

See how strange a crab's eyes look! They are set on **pegs**; some call them **stalks**. The crab can push the eye-pegs out and pull them in. How odd would you look if you could make your eyes stand out six inches? When crabs go into their houses, they draw down their eyes and tuck in their feet.

God made crabs with many different colors. He made some that are red, brown, green, yellow, or blue. The claws of crabs are often of a very bright color. The color on their outer "shells" is less bright; this color is in small dots. The color on some kinds of crabs is in lines. No crab is clear, bright red when it is alive. When crabs are cooked in boiling water, their color turns to bright red. Why is this? We cannot tell why the heat makes their color change.

Mr. Crab and His House

The water from the sea comes and goes in **tides**. Twice each day the water rises—this is called high tide. After each high tide, the water goes back—this is called ebb tide. Each tide lasts six hours. If a stream or brook near your home were high and low twice each day, the change would be like the high and low tides of the sea. If you live near the **ocean**, then you know how the tides flow in and out every day.

When the tide is low, Mr. Crab digs out his house. He scoops out the sand with his big claw. Then he folds his claw to carry the sand, as you would carry grass or leaves in your arm. Some kinds of crabs carry sand in three of their legs, bent to form a basket. Mr. Crab takes the sand

to the top of his hole. Then, with a jerk, he throws the sand in a heap.

Mr. Crab is very strong. He can lift and carry things larger than his body. He digs out a long hall in the sand. He makes rooms in his house. Then he goes with his wife to look for food.

Mr. and Mrs. Crab eat flies, gnats, ants, ladybugs, and other little insects. They also eat seaweed. When beach fleas land on the sand or seaweed, the crabs jump at them and catch the fleas as cats catch mice. Even cats do not move as quickly as Mr. and Mrs. Crab. They put the bugs they catch into their pantry.

Mr. and Mrs. Crab keep near their home in case there is danger. For six hours, while the tide is high, they stay in their house and eat insects and seaweed they have stored away.

God the Creator gave crabs the ability to know how the tides come and go. The crabs know when the tide will be high over their house and when it will be low, so they can come out again.

More About Mr. Crab

I could tell you many strange things about Mr. Crab. At this time, let me simply ask you a question. Where is your **skeleton**? It is inside your body. Your skeleton is made up of bones that hold up your soft flesh. Mr. Crab's "skeleton," however, is on the outside of his body; it is called his **exoskeleton**. It is a thin, hard "shell" that covers Mr. Crab's body. His exoskeleton is like armor that keeps him from being hurt.

Did you know that Mr. Crab can live and breathe either in the water or on the land?

You can live only on the land, but he can live on the land and in the water.

A hen, you know, lays eggs, one by one, in a nest. She keeps them warm till the chicks come out. Mrs. Crab also lays eggs but does not leave them in a nest. She puts her eggs in a long tube or sack. Mrs. Crab carries them tied on her long legs or under her body. When the small crabs come out of the eggs, they grow very fast.

Did you ever try to catch a crab? At first, it will pinch you, if it can, with its big claw. When you catch a crab by its leg and do not let go, it will drop off its leg and run. Could you run with one leg gone? No, but the crab can. In fact, the crab has legs

to spare. When one leg drops off, a new leg will grow back. A boy or girl could never grow a new arm or leg! A crab's leg, however, will grow again very soon.

If a crab's eye-peg is cut off, however, it takes a whole year for a new eye to grow. I think a crab knows that; it is very careful of its eyes.

Mr. Crab has a wide, flat exoskeleton with a notch in each side. He can let his eye-pegs lie in the notches. How can he do that? His eye-pegs are so long he can bend them down flat to fit in the notches. There they are kept safe.

Mr. and Mrs. Crab Get a New Coat

Your skin is soft and stretches easily into a new shape. As you grow more and more, your skin does not break. Your skin gets larger as your body grows. Mr. Crab, however, is in a hard exoskeleton that will not stretch. When it gets too tight, what can Mr. Crab do? What do you do when your coat is too small?

Now I will tell you something strange. When Mr. Crab finds that his "coat" is too small, he takes it off, as you would take off your coat. He pulls his legs, claws, and back out of it. He does that in his house, just like you do when you change your clothes in your room. As Mr. Crab slips out of his exoskeleton, he pulls out his "feet" and claws, as if he were taking off boots and gloves. Then he becomes a helpless, cold creature. His body is only covered with a skin, soft as paste; this skin is made of **lime** and a kind of "glue." In a few days it gets hard. It is as big as Mr. Crab and fits his shape well. It is a strong, new "coat"! It also has the right

colors—blue, brown, red, or gold. It may have spots and rings, too.

When Mrs. Crab changes her "coat," Mr. Crab stays near and tries to keep her from being hurt. He also watches over the young crabs, which have to change their "coats" often. They grow so fast!

Crabs that live in dark mud have dark brown or green exoskeletons. Some crabs have sand-colored ones—pale gray or brown, with close, fine specks like sand on them. God gives each kind of crab just the right color it needs to hide when there is danger.

There are more kinds of crabs than you could count. They live in all parts of the world. This book tells you only about a few of them.

What Mr. Crab Does

Do you get angry quickly? Mr. Crab does, and he also likes to fight. He is like a boy who acts badly when he is upset. When Mr. Crab sees some other crab near his house, he becomes angry. Then he stands high on his toes and pulls in his eye-pegs for fear they will be hurt. He spreads out his big claw. Now Mr. Crab is ready to fight! He runs at his enemy! Each crab tries to hit the other with his big claw. This big claw can cut and pinch hard.

Sometimes Mr. Crab cuts off the claw or leg of the other crab, or he bites the exoskeleton on the other crab's back. If only a leg is cut off, the crab may keep on fighting; but if his claw, eye, or back is hurt, he must give up. He runs home to hide until a new eye, claw, or leg can grow. If your hand is cut off, will it grow again? No, God only gives a few wild

animals the ability to grow new body parts. When Mr. Crab has lost a leg or claw, and a new one grows, it is small at first. Then when he gets a new "coat," the new claw or leg becomes half as large as the one he lost. The next new "coat," the new claw or leg comes out the full size it should be. When Mr. Crab gets a new exoskeleton, we say he **molts**.

When Mr. Crab is afraid, he runs home; but he is very brave and does not fear other crabs. He fears birds most because they eat small crabs, and he cannot fight a bird that is larger than he is.

Swing a rag over a crab's head. Up fly its eye-pegs! Up comes its big claw! There, it has caught the rag! It will not let go. You can lift it into the air by the rag, and it still holds on. Once I saw a blue crab catch a dog's tail. The crab held on fast. The dog gave yelps, and ran up and down the beach. We had to catch the dog and pry open the crab's claw.

Let us look at the crab that grabbed the rag. It has let go of the rag and has gone to dig in its house. If you lay a piece of shell on its hole, it will run up and hit the shell with its head. See it shake! Now it waits. Watch carefully. There, the shell flies up in the air! As the crab ran, it struck the shell hard and made it fly up. I saw the crab try twice, making the shell shake, before it found how hard it must hit the shell to get it out of the way.

Some folks think the crab shuts the door of its house with its big claw. I do not think so. It knows that the tide will wash a lump of sand over its hole for a door. The tide shuts it in. The crab watches the waves come near. At the last wave, it flies into its house because it knows the next wave will close the door. The crab never stays up one wave too long. It gets in its house just in time.

Food for Mr. Crab

The crab that has one large claw has many names. Some call it the "fighting crab" because it is angry so much of the time. Others name him the "calling crab" because, when it runs, it holds its big claw high as if it is calling, "Come! come!" Most people call him the "fiddler crab" and say that its big claw is its **fiddle**. I think **fiddler crab** is the best name for it because it can, and does, play a tune on that claw. Do you see a row of little knobs on the inner edge of its big claw? It rubs those knobs on the edge of the exoskeleton that covers its back and makes a tune. It uses that tune to call its mate, which thinks it is fine music. The crab's big claw is its **violin**, as well as its "hand," "spade," and "sword."

Mr. Crab finds food on the beach, as well as down deep in the sand and in the water. When he walks along the sand, he meets big flies with two wings. He is glad to see them. Why? These flies put their **grubs**, or young ones, in the sand, and Mr. Crab knows just where he can find them to eat. Mr. Crab also meets a large, green **tiger beetle**. He does not fight with him, but Mr. Crab knows that he shall find the beetle's grubs in the sand and eat them.

While he digs down in the sand, he meets a little, fat, round crab with big eyes and a thin, gray exoskeleton. He is glad to see him. If Mr. Crab does not have enough food to eat when the tide is high, he will creep along in the sand and catch this small crab for his dinner. Deep down, Mr. Crab also meets long worms that are green, red, or brown; but he does not trouble them. They are making houses for themselves.

Out in the sea, Mr. Crab finds some small shellfish called **limpets**; they are small snails with flat shells. He likes the limpets so much that he lets them live on his back. They grab a firm hold on his back, and he does not pull them off.

Some Other Crabs

All crabs are not alike. There are many different kinds. They differ in shape, color, and habits. Some are not at all pretty, but others are very beautiful. Some crabs make houses in the sand, while others live in holes in the rocks. All are very special and fun to study.

The **spider crab** has long, thin legs. The front of its exoskeleton, which is over its head, is not wide but comes to a sharp point. This point helps it dig its way into sand and mud.

Spider Crab

The **horseshoe crab** has a chestnut color. Look at its picture at the bottom of the page. Its exoskeleton is in the shape of a horse's hoof with a long tail that has sharp points on the edges. The tail is as hard as wood, and its edges are like a file. The horseshoe crab lives in the sand or mud. It chooses the muddy banks where rivers or streams run into the sea. It pushes its way into the mud with its big, round exoskeleton and scrapes the mud out with its many "feet." The horseshoe crab eats the worms that it finds in the sand and mud. Why are the worms down there? Like the horseshoe crab, they build a house in the mud. Some time I will tell you about these worms.

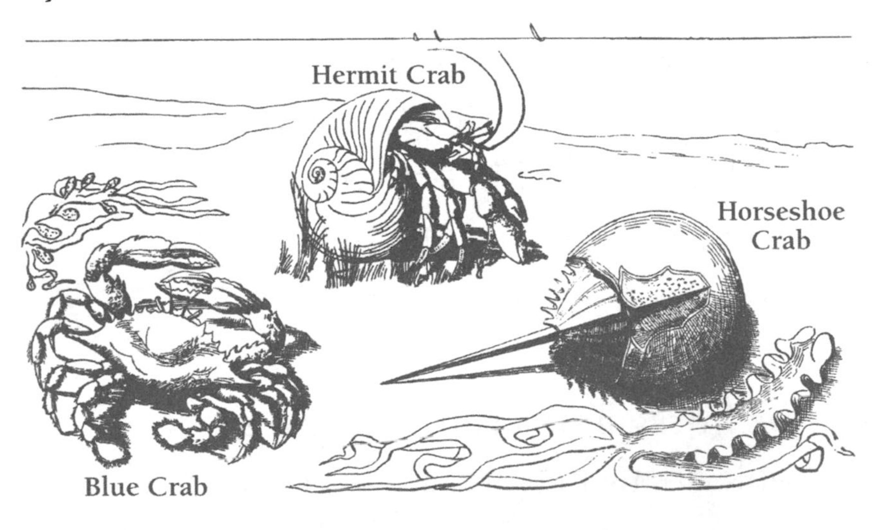

Now and again, as the horseshoe crab goes along under the ground, it finds in its way a long, soft thing that looks good to eat. It is the long pipe, or tube, which a **clam** uses to take in its food. The horseshoe crab puts out its claw to get it. It can move its claw as quickly as a cat can jump or strike out its paw, but the clam is far quicker than the horseshoe crab and shuts its shell down on the crab's claw. Now the crab's claw is caught, like a rat in a trap! It waits to see if the clam will let go. No, it will not. Then the crab drops off its claw and goes away to hide and grow a new one.

In the picture at the bottom of page 16, do you see a crab in a shell made like a curl? That crab steals its house. It finds an empty shell and goes into it to live. It is odd to see this crab run with the shell it stole on its back. How does this crab live? It lives by fishing. In fact, all crabs hunt and fish. You already learned how the crab hunts on the sand for bugs and flies and how it hunts for grubs and worms in the sand. Now it is time for me to tell you how the crab fishes. First, it gets into a good place to fish and pops out its eye-pegs to see all around it. Then, when things that the crab likes to eat float by, it strikes out with its big claw. It catches what it wants nearly every time. The great Creator gave crabs the ability to be good "fishermen."

The Hermit Crab

Do you wish to hear more about the crab that steals its house? Why does it do that? Its back is long and soft, not hard like the backs of other crabs. If it cannot find a hard cover, it will die. Other crabs would bite or pinch it. So would many fish. It is

called the **hermit crab**. As the hermit crab grows too big for one shell, it finds another. It never leaves its shell until it knows that it is about to die. How does it know that? I cannot tell how; only God knows for sure. Even so, it comes out, lies down flat by its house, and dies. The hermit crab wants its house to live in, not to die in.

When the hermit crab needs to change its shell house, it hunts for one that will fit. Then the crab puts its long claw into the shell to feel if it is clean and empty. At times, the hermit finds another crab living in the shell it wants, so the two fight for it. Likewise, if some small creature lives in that shell, the crab pulls it out with its long claw. Then the hermit brings the new shell near and springs from the old shell into the new one, as you would spring from chair to chair.

On the end of its long, soft tail, the hermit crab has a hook. It twists its soft body into the new shell. Then it clasps its tailhook to a small, round post in the top of the curl of the shell. That holds the crab firmly in place. Its horny legs hang out in front; it uses them to run and carry the shell. It can also draw back into the shell and hide if there is danger.

One kind of hermit crab loves a small, pink sea creature that looks like a flower. The crab wants it to grow on its shell. Perhaps it helps the crab catch food or hides the door of the crab's shell. This sea creature can also build more shell on the edge of the one the crab lives in. This makes the shell larger, so the crab does not need to move as often. When it does move, the crab takes its friend along. It puts out its claw and lifts the sea creature off its old shell and sets it on the new one. Then the crab holds it there until it has made itself secure. Then, tail first, the crab slips into its new shell. The fine red, pink, and white frills of its friend hang like a **veil** over its door. They keep fish and other foes away because these frills can sting.

Once I found a nice shell that was empty, so I thought. I kept it for eight or nine days in a box; then I laid it on a shelf. One day I heard, "Clack! Clack! Clack!" There was my shell running up and down the shelf!

In the South Seas some of these crabs do not live in sea shells; they live in coconut shells. They eat the meat of the nuts, and when it is all eaten, they look for another shell. Each night these crabs crawl into the water to get wet. They leave their eggs in the water to **hatch**.

The Crab's Enemies

Crabs have many enemies. Fish and birds eat them. Men eat some kinds of crabs. Crabs eat each other. With so many enemies, crabs would soon be all gone, if they did not lay so many eggs. Each year, a crab lays more eggs than you could count. Crabs do not always have hard shells. When they first come from their eggs, they have long tails, four legs, and no claws. At this time, their bodies have thin covers over them, but they can swim well.

A little, pink crab, named "**pea crab**," goes to live in the shell of the oyster. The oyster does not seem to mind it. You may see this little crab in your oyster soup. It turns orange colored when it is cooked. The **pinna**, or pea crab, has a very soft exoskeleton.

The **spider crab** has a brown "coat," or exoskeleton, that is rough like sand. It has little thorns all over it. This spider crab cuts off fine seaweed with its little sharp claws and hangs it like ribbons on these thorns or hooks. Then it looks like a little green grove! Who can tell why it does that? Is it to hide?

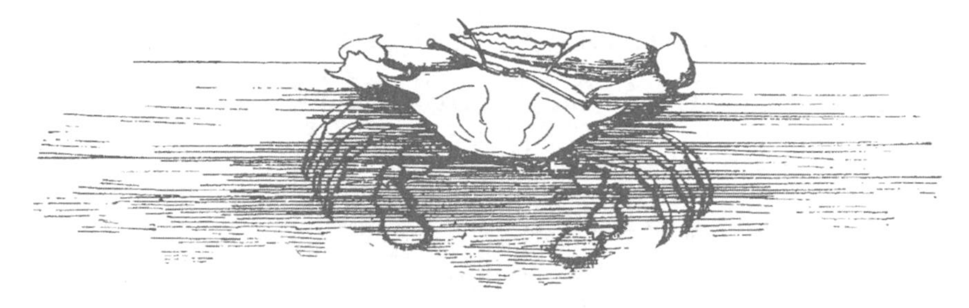

Do you see the wide hind feet of the **blue crab** in this picture? Those are its "paddles," or "oars." They are its swimming "feet." Its exoskeleton is wide and light. This crab can float on the waves like a boat, and it goes far out on the deep sea.

Sand crabs can dig into the sand very fast. They go in backwards. They slip out of sight like a flash, or they leave the tips of their heads and their eye-pegs out to look around. They do this almost every day. Their pale brown or sand-colored "coats," or exoskeletons, are wide and round behind and come to a point in the front. Their heads are in the narrow part of their rough "coats." They are swift runners. God protects sand crabs with their sandy color. When they are afraid, they lie flat on the sand, so it is hard to see them. Even so, some birds have long, thin bills, which they use to pick a crab right out of its sand house.

The Uses of Crabs

How often does a crab get a new coat? Its coat does not wear out, but it gets too small. Then the crab "changes" it to get a larger one.

A baby crab grows fast. It seems to grow before your eyes. You grow fast, too. Your parents say it is hard to keep you in clothes. Your father may be able to wear his coat for many years, but you cannot wear the same coat you had last year. It is the same with a baby crab. When it is very young, it grows fast. It needs a new coat, or exoskeleton, very often. When the crab is older, it grows more slowly. Then it gets a new coat every spring. At last, it does not grow any more but keeps the same coat, year after year. The crab's exoskeleton gets very hard and thick and loses its bright color. Very often it is nearly covered with limpets, or small snails. They fasten their flat or pointed bodies to the crab's back and stay there.

Of what use are crabs? Did God create them for a reason? Yes, the great Creator made all things for a special reason. Sometimes we cannot find out their use, but we do know that crabs are good for food. Some people like to eat certain kinds of crabs—as well as fish, oysters, and other seafood. Birds also like to eat a great many crabs; some birds almost live on them. Many crabs are eaten by fish, too. There are many kinds of crabs so small that you could hardly see them. Fish feed on these small ones, and then men catch and eat the fish.

We also know that crabs help to keep the sea and the seashore clean. Crabs are greedy. They eat nearly all kinds of dead things that would spoil and make a bad

smell if left on the sand. Crabs eat dead fish and dead animals that are thrown into the sea. Do you ever see men going about to clean the streets? In the same way, crabs help to keep the sea and the shore clean. There are so many crabs that they are able to eat a lot of dead fish and animals and do it quickly. This is why they can clean away much of the dead stuff that lies along the shore.

Review

1. Where, and how, does Mr. Crab make his house?
2. Tell me about a crab's eyes.
3. Where is your skeleton? Where is Mr. Crab's "skeleton"? Will you tell me how Mr. Crab gets on his new "coat"?
4. Tell me some of the kinds of crabs that you have studied. What do crabs eat?
5. Why does one kind of crab steal a shell?
6. How do little crabs grow?
7. How did God create the crab that likes to swim in the deep sea?
8. What is a sea tide? How many tides are there each day?
9. When they are afraid, where do crabs hide? What animals catch and eat crabs?
10. Of what use are crabs?

Chapter Two
All About Wasps

Mrs. Wasp and Her Home

Here is a round hole on the hillside path. Is it a crab's hole? No, it is too far from the sea for a crab. Mrs. Wasp made it for her baby to live in. Her name is Vespa. In her house she has a hall, room, and a bed. In the bed her baby lies asleep. It is now a soft, white egg.

When the baby wasp comes out of the egg, it will be all alone. When Mrs. Wasp has laid the egg safe in bed, she goes away. Before she goes, however, she leaves her

baby some food to eat. The food is a pile of little **caterpillars**. Then she shuts the door with a lump of mud. When she leaves her baby, she never comes back. When the baby gets big, it digs its way out and flies off with its four wings. If it meets its mother, the wasp does not know her.

Mrs. Wasp makes her baby's paper bed from tiny bits of wood. She chews the wood up soft and fine in her mouth. She has two small, sharp "saws," which she uses to cut the wood. She chews the wood into a fine dust. Then she mixes it with "glue" from her mouth, and this becomes "paste." This is what she uses to make the paper bed. When she takes the paste home, she spreads it out thinly with her feet. It dries into fine, gray paper. With it, she papers her house to keep her baby warm and dry.

God is very wise. He gave Mrs. Wasp a long stinger, which she uses to gather food for her baby. She kills, or puts into a deep sleep, the caterpillars that she takes home. She is never idle and always works hard.

What Mrs. Wasp Can Do

Do you remember how Mrs. Wasp makes paper? First, she finds a piece of dry, old wood. She cuts off tiny bits of it, like fine, soft threads. She wets these with a kind of "glue" from her mouth and rolls them into a ball. Then, she stands on her hind legs and, with her front feet, puts the ball between her jaws. She then flies to her nest. She uses her tongue, jaws, and feet to spread the ball out thinly. On her hind legs, she has flat feet that help her to lay down the paper. She lays one sheet of paper on another until it is thick enough to make a nest.

Some wasps hang their paper nests in trees or against the side of a building. The wasps that build nests in a tree do not live alone. Some even make nests of pasteboard. Their nests are round like balls or are the shape of a top. At the bottom of each, you will find two doors.

In her home, Mrs. Wasp has many, many paper rooms. They are like cells in a honeycomb. She can make wax. She puts a wax lid on the cells. She can also make **varnish** to keep the cells dry.

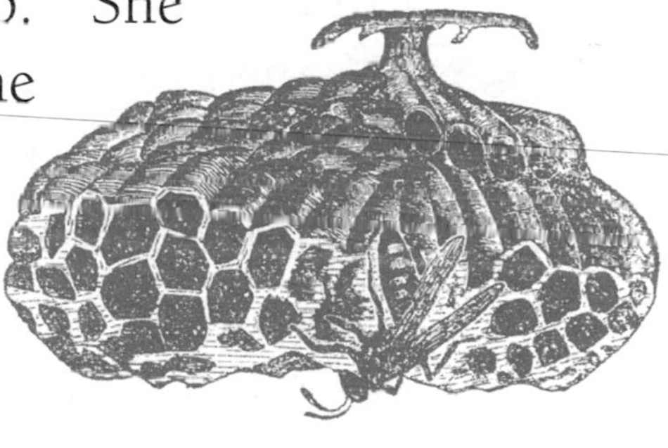

A hornet is a kind of wasp. We may call him Mrs. Wasp's cousin. Hornets catch and eat flies.

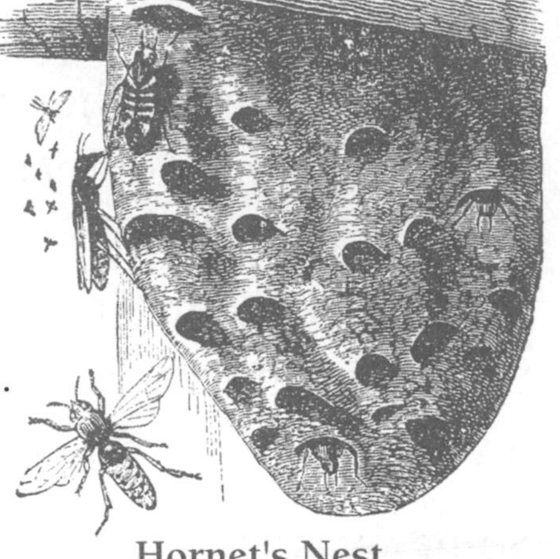
Hornet's Nest

One kind of wasp is a **mason**. Her house is made of mud. She brings mud in little balls and builds a house. In the house, she puts a baby wasp. She puts in little spiders for him to eat.

Mason Wasp

There is a black wasp that is called a **mud dauber**. This kind of wasp does not leave her baby alone. She builds a little mud house. One of these mud wasps built a house on a man's deck. Ten times he broke it up, but she rebuilt it each time. I know a boy who broke one of these mud houses thirty-two times!

The wasp did not give up; she built it up each time.

A Look at Mrs. Wasp

Mrs. Wasp's color is blue-black, and she has yellow marks. All wasps, however, are not of the same color. There is one kind of wasp that is a rust-red color.

Mrs. Wasp has four thin wings—two are large and two are small. The front wings are the large ones. Her wings lie close to her sides when her body is at rest. The wasp looks as if she has two wings, not four. The two bottom wings are hooked to the upper ones.

What does Mrs. Wasp have on her head? She has large eyes that are set close to her head. They have notches or dents in them. She also has two long feelers, called **antennae**, on her head. These feelers are made of twelve or thirteen joints. She touches things with them.

She also has jaws, which she uses to cut up wood for paper.

Mrs. Wasp does not need jaws to eat food because she eats honey. When disturbed, she gets angry and may even kill bees for their honey. Sometimes, she bites into fruit, which spoils it. Likewise, when her baby eats spiders and caterpillars, it does not chew them. It sucks out their "juice."

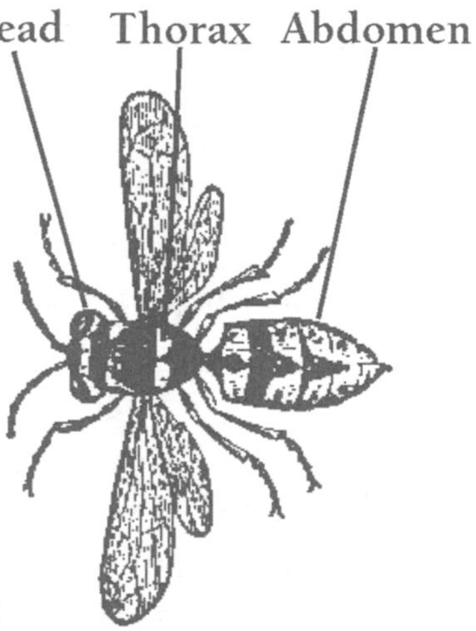

God made Mrs. Wasp's body in three parts. The first part is the **head**, with the eyes, feelers, and mouth. Next is the thick, short middle part called the **thorax**. The third part is the long, slim back end, or **abdomen**. The last two parts join at a point. It looks as if the back end might drop off, but it never does. Mrs. Wasp's body is hard and made of rings like scales.

Head Thorax Abdomen

She also has six legs and four wings, which are set on the thorax. She uses her front legs for hands, and sometimes she stands up on her back legs. Do you remember why she does this? This helps her to roll the bits of wood and paste them into a ball so she can make paper.

Mrs. Wasp has a long, sharp stinger in her tail, or abdomen. The wasp's stinger is like a fine saw with sharp "teeth" on both sides. The tip of the stinger is much sharper than the point of a pin or needle! A drop of poison, which comes from a small sac, runs through the stinger. You do not need to fear Mrs. Wasp, though; she does not sting if you let her alone.

Point of a Pin

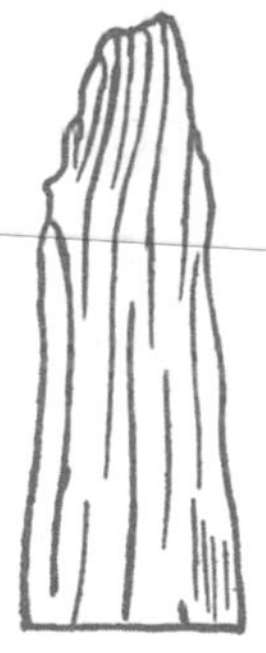

Point of a Needle

Stinger of a Wasp

Mrs. Wasp Cares for Her Babies

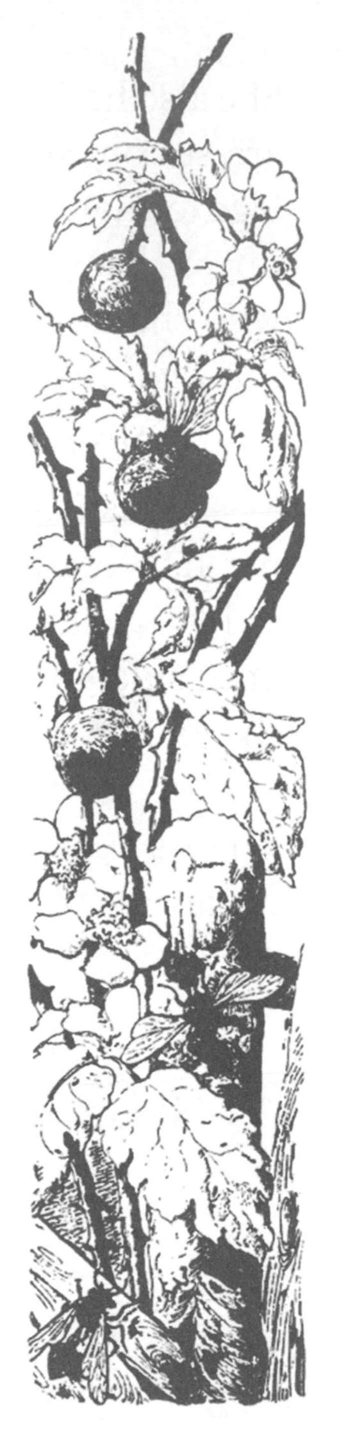

I will now tell you about a wasp that does not live alone. This Mrs. Wasp takes good care of her babies. She is called the **social wasp**.

While it is winter, Mrs. Wasp hides. She does not like the cold weather. Most wasps die in the winter. Only a few live to come out in the spring. The first thing Mrs. Wasp does in the spring is to build a new house. She does not use an old house. She puts her eggs into her house with some food for her babies to eat when they **hatch**.

After the young wasps grow up and come out, they help build. More cells are put into the house. An egg is laid in each cell. The egg grows into a **grub**. Then the wasps feed it. They bring it honey.

The baby wasps have no wings or feet. They need to be closed up to grow into true wasps. When the time comes, the wasps put a wax lid upon each cell. At last the new wasps eat off the lids and come out as full-grown wasps.

Wasps work hard all the time. They fly around looking for food and for things to make paper, wax, varnish, and glue. They have homes to build and little wasps to raise.

When the frost comes, they seem to know they will nearly all die. When the cold begins, the adult wasps look into the cells. They kill all the eggs, grubs, and half-grown wasps that they find there. Why do they do that? They kill them quickly to keep them from dying of hunger and cold. Insects like wasps have some strange ways to care for their young ones.

Remember that a wasp does not grow after it gets its wings and leaves its cell. When it is a fat, round, wingless grub, it is called a **larva**. When the larva stops eating and begins to rest, it is called a **pupa**; this is when the baby wasp slowly changes into an adult. We say a wasp goes through **complete metamorphosis**; this means it completely changes form. Other insects, such as the grasshopper, go through **incomplete metamorphosis**. The grasshopper hatches from its egg as a **nymph**. It looks like an adult grasshopper, but it has to keep changing until it gets its wings.

"Metamorphosis," "larva," "pupa," and "nymph" are hard words to say; but if you practice saying them, you will learn them very quickly. Remember that "ph" makes the sound of the letter "f."

Mrs. Wasp at Home

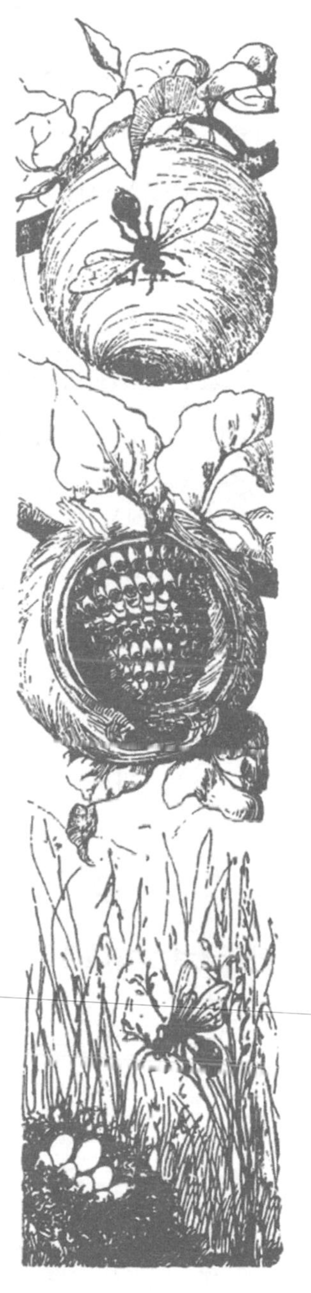

Each kind of wasp makes a different kind of home. There are mud wasps that make mud houses. There are sand wasps that make tiny earth houses on walls and fences. There are also tree wasps that hang large paper houses upon the branches or twigs of trees.

There are **solitary wasps** that build alone in the ground and dig holes in the sand. These wasps throw the sand back between their hind legs as they work. Did you ever see your dog dig a hole? These lonely wasps dig in the same way as a dog.

Rust-red wasps do not build houses for their cells. They make fine paper cells and hang them with the open part down, in some safe place. They varnish the cells to keep them dry.

In cold lands, wasps build nests in barns, attics, hollow trees, or in the ground. In warm lands, they hang a **cluster** of cells out in the open air, on trees or vines.

One day I found a wasp's nest in an old tin can. There had been paint in the can. Mrs. Wasp had used the old paint to make a stem. She used her feet to twist the paint into a stiff "rope." On this stem, she built a nest in the shape of a flower. First, she put one cell upon the stem; then she placed six cells around the first one. In each cell, she laid a tiny, white egg.

Soon the eggs grew into fat grubs with black heads, and Mrs. Wasp began to feed them. She went from one cell to the other and fed her grubs, just as a bird feeds its young. Mrs. Wasp made a pap, or soft food, of bugs and fruit and gave it to her young.

Wasps are very neat. They keep their nests clean. They use cells more than once, but they always make new nests each year. All wasps have a clean, shining coat and a fierce look. Wasps do not make a mess when they eat because they do not bite or chew food. Do you remember how they eat? They suck out the juices of fruit and insects.

Review

1. What is a wasp? How many legs and wings does a wasp have?
2. How do a wasp's antennae help it?
3. Name the three parts of a wasp's body.
4. Why do the two wings on each side of a wasp's body seem like one?
5. What things can wasps make? Tell me how wasps make paper.
6. What kind of houses do wasps build? Give the name for each kind of wasp.
7. What can you say about a wasp's stinger?
8. How does a social wasp care for her babies?
9. How do baby wasps grow? What are the different names given to a wasp as it grows?
10. How does the wasp eat?

Chapter Three
All About Bees

The Bees and Mr. Huber

Did you ever see a hive of bees? Do you know how small the bees are? Are you afraid of bees? You need not be afraid of them. They do not often sting those who let them alone. There are some people whom bees never sting. As you may already know, bees move very quickly and live in a hive.

Now I will tell you a strange thing. The man who knew most about bees was a blind man! His name was Mr. Huber. He lost his eyesight when he was a boy. Mr. Huber loved to study. Most of all, he loved to study bees.

When Mr. Huber was a boy, he had a friend. She was a kind girl. She, too, loved to study. When she grew up, she became

Mr. Huber's wife. They were not poor but had a nice home of their own. Mr. Huber also had a man to live with him and serve as his helper.

Mr. and Mrs. Huber and the servant would go and sit by a **beehive**. They read to Mr. Huber all the books about bees that had been written at that time. They would also watch the bees to see if they did the things that were described in the books. When they saw the bees do other things, they told Mr. Huber. Then they caught bees and studied the parts of their bodies. They used a **magnifying glass** to see the bees up close.

His wife and servant told Mr. Huber all that they saw. They watched the bees, year after year. Mr. Huber studied them for fifteen years, and then he made a great book about them. He told his wife what to write, and she wrote everything on paper. He lived to be very old and wise in the ways of bees.

You may learn more about bees by reading books and by watching bees with your own eyes. Ask God to help you to study the habits of bees very carefully.

The Bee Colony

There are many different kinds of bees. The one that is known the best is the honeybee; it lives in a **colony**. Do you know what this bee makes for you to eat? If you said honey, you are right. It makes honey from the **nectar**, or sweet juice, of flowers. Honey is used as food and is stored in the beehive.

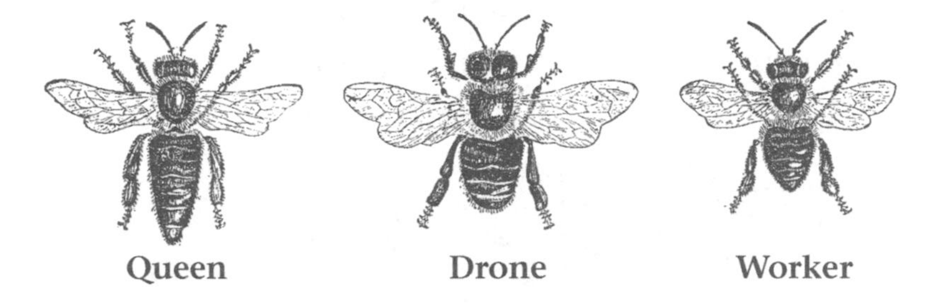

Queen Drone Worker

Each colony, or hive, has three types of bees—queen, drone, and worker bees. There is one **queen** in each hive, and she rules over all the other bees. She is the mother of all. Her main work is to lay eggs in the cells; she may lay 1,200 or more eggs in a day! The queen has a small stinger that she can use over and over again. She may live five or six years.

The male bees are called **drones**. There are hundreds of them in each hive, but they hardly do any work. They are so helpless that they must be fed. Some say that they mostly play and walk around all day. Drones have large eyes, strong wings, and wide bodies; but they do not have stingers. They live about forty-five days.

Who, then, builds so many fine cells? Who stores up all the honey? Who feeds the baby bees? The small, quiet, brown **workers** do all that. There are more worker bees than you can count to do all the hard jobs; some say there are 50,000 workers in each hive! Worker bees live about four months in the winter but only six weeks in the summertime.

The worker bees make honey, **beebread**, and **royal jelly**, which they feed to the

baby bees. Beebread is a mixture of pollen, honey, and bee **saliva**. Royal jelly is like beebread but has more honey and saliva mixed in it. Some workers gather nectar and pollen; others stand guard to protect the colony from enemies. In the fall, the worker bees push all the drones out of the hive into the cold to die. In winter, the workers cluster around the queen to keep warm and to eat honey.

Bee Larvae

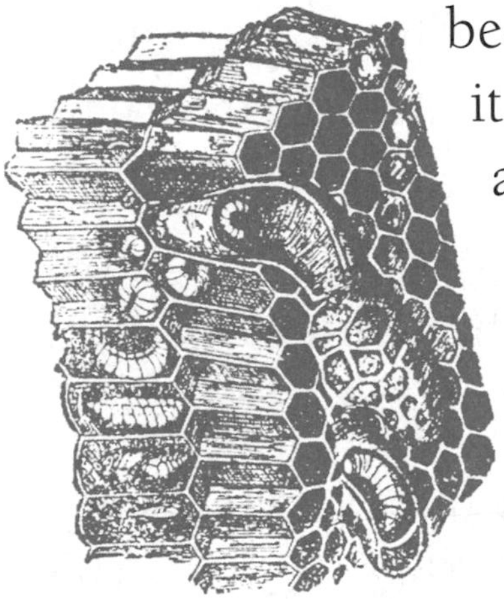

How does a bee grow? The bee is first an **egg**. Then it hatches and becomes a grub, or **larva**. Then, closed in its cell, the **pupa** grows legs and wings and turns into a full-grown **adult**. When a bee goes through all of these changes, it is called **metamorphosis**.

A bee has three body parts—head, thorax, and abdomen. Its parts are put close together, and its body looks like it is held together with rings. The bee has six legs, four wings, and many eyes set close together; its eyes look like one large eye. The bee also has many hairs on its legs and body. These fine hairs are its velvet coat. The bee also has a mouth with a long tongue. It rolls out its tongue to get nectar from flowers.

The queen bee has a long, slim body and small wings. She can sting, and so can a worker bee. The drone bee has a thick body, a round head, and no stinger. The worker bee is not as large as the other two, but it has strong wings. The worker bee must fly far to get nectar, pollen, water, or "tree gum." But the queen bee usually stays at home.

Worker Bees

When young worker bees first come out of their cells, they are usually **nurse bees**—they take care of the larvae. They also keep the hive cool with their wings. These bees can make wax, too. The wax comes out from under the scalelike bands on their tail ends. The wax is made inside the bees from the nectar that they eat.

Each worker bee has two **stomachs**. In them, it puts the nectar that it gets from flowers. The bee takes the nectar in one stomach home and puts it into some of the cells. It holds nectar in the other stomach to eat and to make wax.

If you look at a worker bee's leg, you will see a "basket," a "brush," and a "tool"—which is used to remove the wax on its tail end. When the bee goes into a flower, it gets covered with yellow dust, or **pollen**. The "brush" on its

Bee's Leg

leg takes off the pollen from the bee's coat and puts it into the "basket." This pollen is used to feed the young bees.

With the "tool," the bee strips the scales of wax from the rings on its body. Then it takes the wax in its mouth and spreads it out to build the wall of a cell. Did you ever see a man lay brick on a wall? The bee builds its wall very much like a man builds his brick wall. When the worker bee makes a cell, it first lays down a thick sheet of wax. On this sheet, it then builds little wax cells—each with six sides set close to each other. When the cells are as deep as the bee wants them to be, it fills them.

With what do the nurse bees fill these cells? Some cells are used to store food, called **beebread**; it is made from pollen and honey. They use other cells to store honey; first they get nectar from flowers, and then they store it in the cells to dry and ripen into honey. Other cells are used for baby bees, or larvae, to grow in. The queen puts one egg in each cell. After the larvae hatch, the nurse bees feed them with royal jelly and beebread.

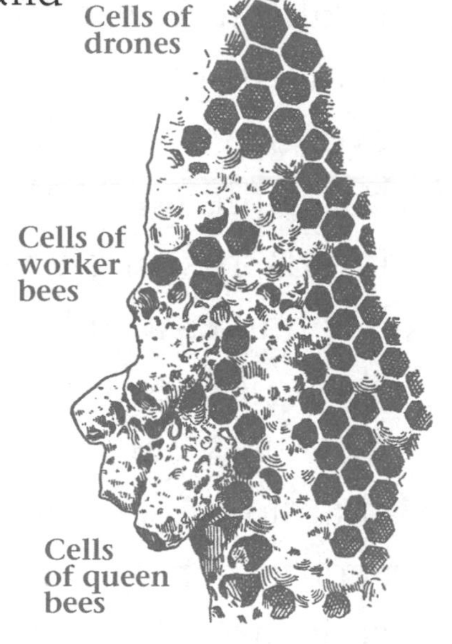

Baby Bees

The worker bees know that some of the baby bees, or grubs, must grow to be queens, some to be drones, and others to be workers.

A baby worker bee grows in a small cell. After three days, a grub hatches from its egg. This grub, or larva, gets **royal jelly** for three days. For three more days, it is fed only **beebread**. When it fills its whole cell, the cell is closed with a cap of wax. Then it turns into a pupa and rests for twelve days. During this time of rest, the pupa changes into an adult worker bee; then it chews its way out of its cell. Do you remember what all these changes are called? It is **metamorphosis**.

For a queen grub, or larva, the nurse bees make a large, round cell—there are five or six cells for queen grubs in each hive. Then the nurse bees feed the baby queen. They give the grub all it can eat of **royal jelly** mixed with more **saliva**. This larva grows large, as it eats more food. After it rests as a pupa, it turns into an adult queen. Then it begins to sing a song, and the old queen bee hears it. She knows that the new queen will soon come out.

There can be only one queen in a hive at one time, so the old queen says, "Come! I will go away! I will not live here any more!" Many of the bees say, "We will go with our queen." Then they fly out of the hive in a cloud. They wish to find a new home. Did you ever see bees **swarm**?

They may fly far away or land nearby. They hang on a vine, tree branch, or stick like a bunch of grapes.

Can you put them into a new hive? Yes, drop them softly into a new hive where there is a piece of honeycomb. In a few hours, they are calm and go to work. The workers begin to make cells. They spread wax and build walls. Young bees lay bits of wax just right, making perfect six-sided cells. God gave them the skill to do this from birth; it is called **instinct**.

Battle of the Queen Bees

After the old queen goes out in a swarm, what do the rest of the bees do? They all keep still, but they look to the cells where the new queens sing. Then one new queen breaks off the lid of her cell and comes out. She lifts her head, spreads her wings, and dries her legs. Her legs are like gold. Her dress is velvet and gold. She looks beautiful! The bees fan her and feed her.

But wait! A cell nearby begins to open and out comes one more new queen! This will not do. Two queens cannot live in one hive. When the two queens see each other, they rush and begin to fight. If they stop to rest, the workers make them keep up the battle. At last, one of them stings the other near the wing and kills her. Then this strong queen runs to the other cells where the baby queens lie. She tears off the wax caps, stings each new queen bee, and then they die.

Now the strong queen is the one true queen of the hive. The worker bees accept her as their new queen.

The queen bee only leaves the hive twice. Once, a few days after she is made queen, the worker bees let her go out for her mating flight. She does not fly far. She has no basket to collect pollen, and she does not need to collect nectar. All she needs to do is to mate with several drones and come home and lay eggs. She does not go out again until she is ready to swarm. Then she leads off a swarm of old bees and leaves the hive to the next new queen bee.

The Worker Bee

Now you know how the new queen bee is born and how she lives. So let us see how the worker bee lives. In its small cell, the worker does not grow as large as the queen bee, but it has stronger wings. When it is fully developed, it chews off the cap of its cell and comes out. It is now able to go to an open cell that is filled with nectar. The new bee eats the nectar and gains strength. The other bees can now touch it with their **antennae** and "talk" to it. They lick it with their tongues, to smooth its brown coat. They also help the bee spread its wings. Now it is ready to begin its work as a nurse bee.

A worker bee cleans, repairs, and defends the hive; it also cares for the baby bees. After about three weeks in the hive, it then becomes a **field bee** and goes to get nectar and pollen. At once, it knows how to do this.

It does not need to learn because God has already given this skill to the young bee; this is called **instinct**. It can find its way to the right flowers, and it tries to keep out of the way of things that will hurt it.

What color do the bees like best? They like blue the best, and then red and purple. They also like sweet smelling flowers and all flowers that have sweet nectar. They bring this nectar home to make honey or wax. They bring home pollen, water, and "tree gum," too.

The field bees get the "tree gum," or **propolis**, from the buds of trees. This sticky material is like glue. It is used to line the cells and make them strong. It is also used to seal any openings in the hive against drafts or invaders.

If a queen bee dies, and all the baby queens are also dead, what can the bees do? They take the tiny larva of a worker bee and make it their queen. Can they continue to live if they have no queen? No, not for long, because there will be no eggs laid. How do they make a queen from a worker bee? They pick out a good grub and put it into a round queen cell. They feed the worker grub "queen food," or royal jelly. When it grows up, it will not become a worker but a queen.

The Wise Bees

In the beehive, all is not peace and joy. Foes come in and try to kill the poor bees. Who are these foes? A **caterpillar** may come into the hive to live, but the bees do not like him. He is not clean, and he gets in their way. **Slugs** may also come in. **Snails** and **moths** come to steal the honey, as well.

When the foe is a small fly or slug, the bees kill it and take it out, but a large

worm or slug they cannot take out. What do they do then? They kill it, if they can, with their stingers. Then over it, they build a grave of wax and "tree gum," or **propolis**. That is to keep the bad smell of the dead creature from the cells.

If a snail comes in, they use this same strong gum, or propolis, to glue him to the floor. Then it must die in its shell. If a strange queen flies in, they will not sting her, but she must not stay. So the worker bees form a ball about her until she dies for lack of air.

Bees have other enemies, too. Some birds like to eat them. Other birds break into the hive to get honey. Bears also like honey and break up wild bees' nests to get it. Hens and toads eat bees, as well; but moths make the worst trouble for the bees.

African Bee Eater

In the fall, the bees are done storing up all the honey they need to eat; they know the flowers are all dead and their nectar is gone. Then the worker bees push all the drones out of the hive, because they do not want to feed them when it is cold. In the winter, bees need to cluster around the queen to keep warm. When they eat the food they have stored up, it also helps them to stay warm. As soon as spring comes, they go out of the hive and go right to work.

Do all bees build in hives? No, wild bees like to build in hollow trees. In hot lands, some bees build in holes in the rock. Swarms of bees that leave hives find odd places to live. I knew of a swarm that found a hole in the roof of a house. The bees got into the roof and lived there five years. When a man took them out, there were two big tubs full of comb. Is it not interesting that so much wax can be made by so many small nurse bees?

Other Bees

Did you ever find in the earth the nest of a **bumblebee**? The bumblebee works hard. It digs a hole in the earth with its front feet. When it has made a hall and a room, the bumblebee makes a nest, which is made of grass or leaves or hay, cut fine. Then it lays eggs in the nest. It makes honey in large combs. The combs are more soft and dark than those which the honeybee makes. Field mice and moles eat these bees and their combs.

The small **carpenter bee** lives alone. It saws out a nest in a post or tree and makes one room over the other. In each room, it puts an egg and food. It seals the door up with a paste made of sawdust. Then it goes off and dies. The next spring, out come the new bees. They know how to get food and make homes, just as their mother did.

Carpenter Bee

The **mason bee** also lives alone. This little, shiny black bee makes nests in small, long holes found in trees, posts, or old walls. First, it gathers food and puts it at the end of a hole. Next, it lays an egg in the cell. After that, it takes its own saliva and mixes it with fine mud or clay to wall off the cell. It makes about five cells in each long hole. Then it begins a new nest.

The **miner bee** lives in a colony. Each female bee builds a tunnel in the ground.

First, it makes about six clay cells in the tunnel. Next, it puts pollen in the cells for its babies to eat. After that, the bee lays one egg in each cell. When the eggs hatch, the baby bees will feast on the food left by its mother.

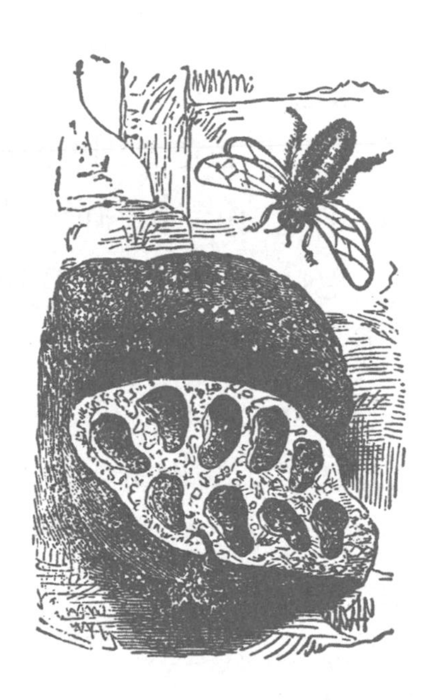

The **burrowing bee** makes a house much like an anthill. First, it makes a long hall. Off the hall, it builds small rooms. Next, in each room, it rolls food in a ball like a pea. Then it lays an egg by the food and leaves the small bee to grow up alone.

One kind of bee is so neat that it does not like to see a mud wall. What do you think it does to make its wall pretty? It cuts out bits of nice, soft leaves or petals and lines its cell with them! At times, it takes bits of green leaves from a plum tree, but it likes bright colors best.

Another kind of bee likes red poppy petals best; it cuts the bits of petal quite small. This bee may also use pink petals from a rose flower. It glues them all over its cell. Then it puts in food and an egg. Don't you think its baby bee will like its pretty, red or pink cell?

The **tree bee** is also called the "wild bee." It finds an old tree with a hollow trunk; cleans out the old, dead wood; and builds nice combs. A tall tree may be full of combs, from root to top. In such a tree, more than one swarm will live and work. Each swarm has its queen, and each colony keeps in its own place.

Also, there is a bee in Brazil that makes a large nest, like a great bag. It is full of round balls; the balls are full of honey. The wax and honey of this bee are of a dark color.

Did you know that smoke makes bees fall, like they were dead? People drive bees off with the smoke from a fire made from wood or paper.

More About Bees

Do you know someone who owns bees? Once I knew a young man who had some bees. He kept them in a room at the top of his house. He left the window open, and the bees came and went as they pleased.

People can buy a swarm of bees for very little money. If they take good care of their bees, they can make money by

selling the bees' honey to their neighbors or local stores.

If you live in the city, you cannot keep bees very easily. Why not? The bees may not find the right food. They need to fly in a field or garden, so they can get the nectar and pollen from the flowers; without them they cannot make honey and beebread. They also need to fly where they can get the thick gum from the buds of trees to line their cells.

If you have a hive of bees, you should learn to watch them closely. If you stand by a hive, the bees will not hurt you if you keep still and do not get in their way, as they go in and out of their hive. Like Mr. Huber, you may find out some new things. We do not yet know all about bees. We could also learn more than is now known about drones. Perhaps, one day, some young beekeeper like you may even write a book about bees!

For the winter, bees store up more honey than they need. So the beekeepers take out much of it to eat or to sell, but they must leave some for the bees. If too much comb is taken out, the bees must be fed. You can give them sugar or some sweet things. Bees also like flour made from sweet peas. I guess you could say that bees have a sweet tooth!

Bees cannot feed young bees if they do not have sweet pollen or flour. They cannot make wax if they do not have sweet nectar. They cannot line their cells, nor seal them well, if they do not have strong gum from tree buds.

I know some people who think bees like to hear a song, and so they sit near the hives and sing to them. Bees really love colors, sweet smells, and nice tastes; they do not care much for any noise.

Review

1. How does the honeybee live? With what does it make honey?
2. What three types of bees live in a hive?
3. What does the queen bee do? What does a drone bee do, and how does he look? Which bee makes the cells?
4. Why do bees gather nectar, pollen, and "tree gum"? What colors do field bees like best? What do bees eat? How do worker bees make wax?
5. How do nurse bees make a queen?
6. Why does a swarm of bees leave the hive? Why do the queen bees fight?
7. In what odd places do bees live?
8. What creatures like to eat the bees and steal their honey?
9. Name other kinds of bees. What do their names tell you about them?
10. How must you take care of bees, if you have them?

Chapter Four
All About Spiders

What is Mrs. Spider like?

It is time, my little friends, to have some fun. We will pretend that we are listening to a real discussion between two young children and a spider. If you keep reading, you will find out what these children learned from Mrs. Spider.

Ashley: To what family of **insects** do you belong, Mrs. Spider?

Mrs. Spider: I am not an insect at all. I belong to a group of small creatures called **arachnids**. Look at my picture and see if there is any difference between it and this picture of a bee.

Ashley: You have eight legs, while the bee has only six; and you do not have any wings, while the bee has four; and there are only two parts to your body, while the bee has three.

Mrs. Spider: Yes, all true insects have only six legs, two or four wings, and three body parts; but arachnids have eight legs, only two body parts, and no wings.

Joshua: Do you lay eggs, and do they hatch as a larva that changes into a pupa?

Mrs. Spider: We lay eggs, but when they hatch, little spiders come out of them right away. We carry and care for our little ones until they are able to care for themselves.

Ashley: Do you have a stinger like the bee and the wasp?

Mrs. Spider: I bite instead of sting; but my bite will not hurt anything except a fly or some other insect. Some of my relatives do hurt when they bite people.

Joshua: Do you have hundreds of eyes, as some insects do?

Mrs. Spider: I have only eight eyes, but they are placed in different parts of my head so that I can see in all directions at once. Many spiders have six eyes, and a few spiders have only two.

Ashley: Are you different from insects in other ways?

Mrs. Spider: Yes, my body is soft and has no hard, horny covering like most insects have. I shed my skin as I grow older and larger, while most insects do not. I am able to run if I lose half of my legs. If I lose a leg, a new one grows out in its place.

Joshua: Are there many kinds of spiders?

Mrs. Spider: There are hundreds of kinds of spiders. They are grouped into five main families, according to their habits, and there may be many different kinds in one family. All belong in one general class called *Arachnida*.

Ashley: What are your family names?

Mrs. Spider: First, **hunting spiders**, which run about hunting their prey; second, **wandering spiders**, so called because they have no homes; third, **prowling spiders**, which run about near their webs to hunt for food; fourth, **sedentary spiders**, which sit much of the time (they like to settle in one place); fifth, **water spiders**, which are also **sedentary**, but live in water instead of on land.

Joshua: What do you like to do during the day?

Mrs. Spider: We can all dive in the water, and some of my cousins can build rafts. We hunt, plant mosses and ferns, and are famous spinners and weavers. We make bridges, balloons, and parachutes. One of my cousins makes a house lined with fine, soft curtains and has a door fastened in place with a hinge. We call him a **trapdoor spider**. A special kind of spider makes a tent to live in, another builds a tower, while another spins silk that is woven into beautiful dresses and ribbons. We can also tell when the weather is going to change.

Ashley: I think Solomon watched spiders in his palace because he said, "The spider taketh hold with her hands, and is in kings' palaces." (Proverbs 30:28)

I hope you learned as much from Mrs. Spider as Ashley and Joshua did!

An insect has six legs, and its body has three parts. At first, an insect is a tiny **egg**. Then a **larva** hatches from the egg and begins to eat and eat. When the larva is ready, it is closed in a cell or case; now it becomes a **pupa**. The pupa slowly turns into a full-grown **adult** with legs and wings. After it comes out of its cell or case, it is as large as it ever will be. An insect does not grow after it gets wings. The small wasp does not grow into a big wasp, nor the small bee into a big bee. The first size they have when they come out is the size that they keep.

The spider, on the other hand, is a creature of another kind. The spider also lays eggs, but out of the eggs come little

spiders that will grow into big spiders. The spider changes its size as it grows. It **molts**, or sheds its skin, as it grows bigger. The body of an insect is hard and is made in rings. It cannot pull its coat off to get bigger, as a crab can.

The spider's body is soft. Its skin is tough, and it changes its skin often when it is very young. The spider has eight legs instead of six, and most spiders have eight eyes. The spider's body is in two parts. To kill its **prey**, God gave it poison, but its poison is not in a stinger in the tail. It is in the base of the two jaws that God wisely created for the spider.

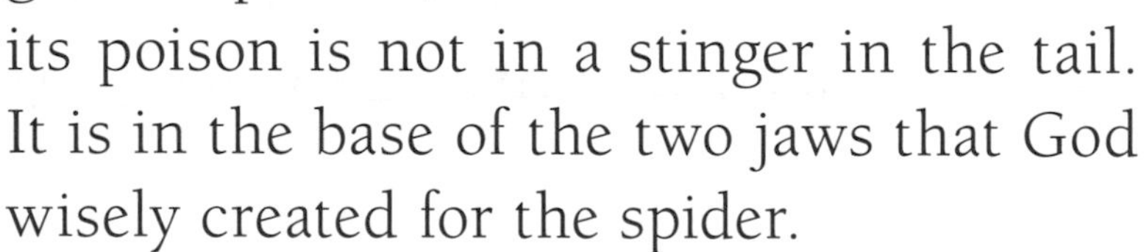

Some spiders are somewhat like crabs, and others are somewhat like insects, such as the **daddy longlegs**—also called the harvestman or harvest spider. The daddy longlegs is like a true spider, but it has an abdomen that is divided into parts. This spider has eight long, slender legs and feeds on small insects.

The front part of a spider's body is not as large as its back part. All eight legs and the head are attached to the front part of the spider. Sometimes a spider is apt to bite off another spider's legs! A spider can live and run when half of its legs are gone; but soon it can grow fine, new legs just like a crab can.

Front End of a Spider

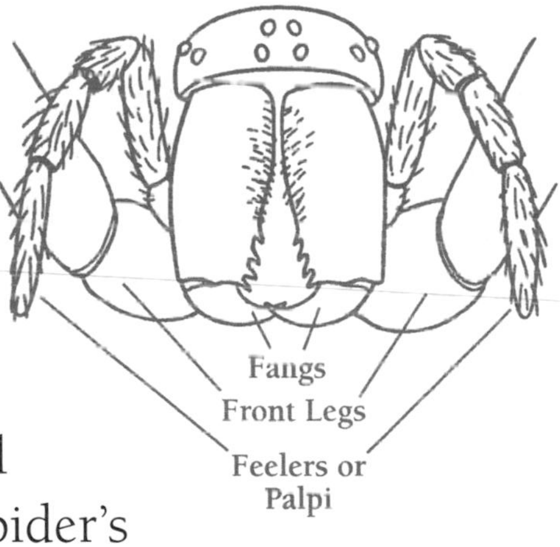

A spider does not have any wings, but it has two small feelers, called **palpi**, which it uses to feel and hold its food. You will also see on the spider's head two short **fangs**, which have poison

Spider's Leg

in them. They are used to bite its prey. A spider also has claws on each of its eight feet; they are very much like a lion's claws. On each claw is a "comb" which keeps the spider from falling when it walks up a wall. It uses its legs to jump, climb, walk, and guide its thread when it spins.

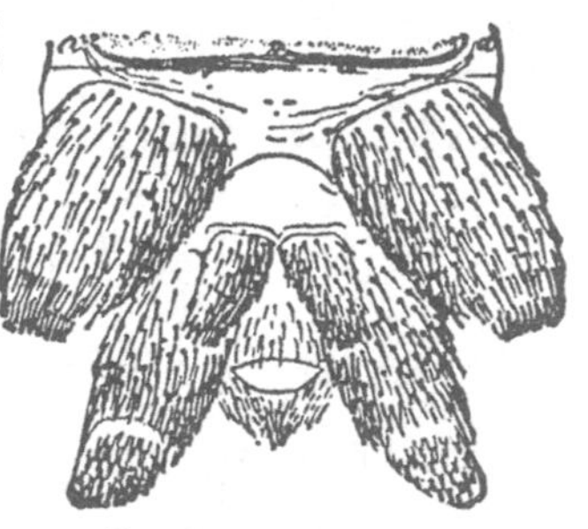
Spinnerets

A spider spins a web using its large, round back part; this part has six small round tubes; they are called **spinnerets**. Each of them is made of many very small tubes. What are these spinnerets used for? They are used to spin a **web**. How does the spider spin its web? In the spinneret is a kind of glue; when it is drawn out into the air, it gets hard. The glue becomes a fine **silk** thread. As it comes out, it is woven into a net that we call a web. All spiders spin webs.

As a spider grows, it pulls off its "coat" like Mr. Crab does. The crab's "coat" is called its **exoskeleton**. A spider also has an exoskeleton; its "coat" is hard and tough. Before a baby spider is two months old, it sheds its "coat" three or four times. We say it **molts** when it does this. It spins a bit of line and holds it firmly. Then the exoskeleton on the front part of its body cracks open; after this, the back part of its exoskeleton falls off. Then, by kicking hard, it gets its legs free. The spider's new "coat" is fine and soft but soon grows firm and tough.

Spiders come in all colors. Their clothes are like velvet. They may be black, brown, red, or gold. They may come in stripes and spots. Spiders are like kings or queens in their rich clothes. Some spiders are so small you can hardly see them. One of the very tiny ones is clear, bright red. Others are very big with poison in their bites. The big ones are black, with spots and stripes, and have thick coats like fur.

The Spider at Home

The spider, like the wasp, is busy all the time, but it is not as angry as a wasp. The bite of a spider usually does not do much harm to a man or a child. A spider does not bite unless it is hurt, or when it kills its prey. Its bite kills flies, bees, wasps, ants, and other insects, to eat.

Spiders can spin, weave, dig, and hunt. Some can build rafts, and others make mud houses. They make webs, nests, and snares.

Their **webs** are used to live or rest. Their **nests** are for baby spiders. Their **snares** are to catch food. The silk of the web is very fine, but it is very strong. It will hold up a big, fat spider, and it will firmly hold a wasp or a bee.

Do you see the spider on its thread? It is the spider's "swing." It can swing as the boy does in his rope swing. Do you see the spider rest in its web? It can rest like the girl in a **hammock** made of string. How does the spider spin its web? First it finds a good place. Then it presses the end of a spinning tube and makes a drop of glue stick to a wall, leaf, or stem.

Then it drops away; and as it goes, the glue spins out in many fine streams that join into one silklike thread. If the spider does not find a good place to make its web hold, it will climb back up!

Silk-spinning Spider

Look at the spider climb. He runs up his line as fast as he came down. If you scare the spider, it drops down on its line like a flash. It will not break. If you break the line, the spider winds up the end quickly. Then it runs off to find a new place in which to make its web. The long lines in the web are called **rays**. The spider spins the rays first. The rays are spread out like the **spokes** of a wheel. Webs come in many shapes. You often see a round web. The spider guides the lines with its feet as it spins. It pulls each line to see if it is firm. Then the spider spins a thread, round and round, from ray to ray, until the web is done.

The Little Nest

Mrs. Spider's web is made from two kinds of **silk**. The silk of the rays is smooth. The silk that goes across the rays has tiny drops of glue on it. This makes the line stick to the rays. Mrs. Spider begins her lines at the outer edge. They are laid closer to each other as she gets to the center of the web. When all is done, she is in the center and does not need to walk on her new web.

Mrs. Spider also has a **nest** near her web. From the nest, she runs a line. She can sit in the door of her nest and hold the line in her claw. When a bug or fly gets caught on the web, the web shakes, and she feels her line move. Then she runs down the line and **stuns** or kills the bug or fly. Then Mrs. Spider

winds some fine web around it. She makes a neat bundle of it, and then she carries it off to her nest to eat. You can make Mrs. Spider run down her line if you shake the web a very little with a blade of grass or a stick. She will run out to see if she has caught a bee or fly.

Mrs. Spider's nest is made of silk thread that is spun close together. It looks like soft, fine cloth. Her nest may be in the shape of a ball, horn, or basket. Each kind of spider makes its nest in the shape it likes best. No more than two spiders ever live in a nest, but most spiders like to live all alone. In the nest, Mrs. Spider lays her eggs in a silk ball. The eggs, at first, are very soft. After a while, they grow harder. When the baby spiders come out of their eggs, they must be fed. Mrs. Spider takes good care of them. They grow fast. When they are full-grown, they go off and make their own webs. At times the eggs are left in the silk ball all winter. The baby spiders come out in the spring. Although their parents are dead, the young ones already know how to hunt and spin.

Very young spiders do not have such rich clothes as older ones do; and the hairs of their coats are not so thick. Their soft, silklike coats, with their rich color, are the only beauty they have. These small spiders will stay by their mother and sit on her back. They act like baby chicks which stay close to their mother, Mrs. Hen. Most spiders live only one year. Some live two years, while others live over four years.

People do not like spiders' long legs and their round, soft, baglike bodies. Still, some people who watch spiders learn to like them very well.

The Spider and His Food

Some people say that they hate spiders; but why do they hate them?

They say, "Spiders are so very greedy!"

Well, a spider must eat a great deal, or it cannot spin its web. The spider's food helps it make the glue that it uses to spin its web. Spiders work hard, so they must eat a lot food.

Others say, "Spiders bite."

They will not bite you, though, if you do not hurt them. If they do, the bite usually will do you no harm. The bite of a **brown spider**, however, can make you very sick. Spiders bite to kill insects, not to hurt people. Do you not eat fish, meat, and birds? Who kills this food for you? A hard working person called a hunter does, of course. The spider is a kind of hunter, too. It hunts insects.

Still others say, "Spiders are not pretty."

But God created many spiders that are very beautiful. And they come in many interesting shapes, sizes, and colors. Look at their fine, black or gold coats! Their webs are very pretty, too.

When flies get caught in a web, they hum loud from fear; then the spiders eat them. Spiders eat other small creatures, as well. Some spiders, called **tarantulas**, may eat mice and other small animals. One kind of tarantula that lives in trees even kills small bats to eat!

There is another kind of spider that lives on water. It knows how to build a raft. It takes grass and bits of stick and ties them up with its silk. On this raft, it sails out to catch flies and bugs that skim over the water. There is another kind of spider that lives in the water; it can dive. Its nest is in the shape of a ball that shines like silver. Its web is so thick that the spider does not get wet. Its velvet coat keeps it as dry as a fur coat. Its eggs are the color of gold!

Mrs. Spider is very neat when she eats. She does not leave crumbs because she does not chew her food; she only sucks out the "juice" of her prey.

Mrs. Spider also hates dust and dirt. She will not have a dirty web. If you put a bit of dirt or leaf on her web, Mrs. Spider will go and clean it off. She shakes her web with her foot until all the lines are clean. If the dirt will not fall off, she will cut out the piece and **mend** the web with new lines.

Other Interesting Spiders

I have told you about some interesting spiders like the **garden spider** that makes the round web. I also told you about the spider that makes a raft and the one that dives. There are many more interesting spiders to learn about, as well.

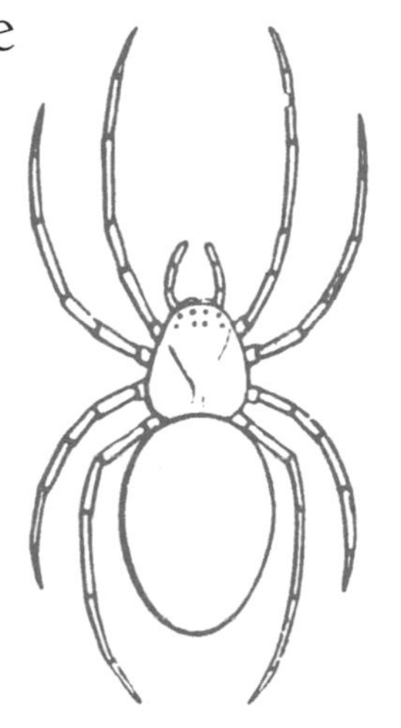

Garden Spider

There is an unusual spider that runs on water. How can it do that? Have you seen boys dash about on ice with skates on their feet? Or did you ever see a man walk on snow with snowshoes? This spider wears "shoes" like that! It has "water shoes" made for walking on the water. What do they look like? They look like small toy balloons that are attached to each of the spider's eight feet. These tiny bags of air keep the spider from sinking.

The **trapdoor spider** is an interesting spider that lives in the ground. It digs a tube down and makes its nest in the earth. At the top of the hole, it makes a door with a hinge that will open and shut. How does the spider make such a door? It spins a thick web and fills it with earth. Then the spider folds the web over to hold the dirt in and makes a hinge of silk thread. The unusual thing is that this spider plants moss or small ferns on its door! It digs the moss up and sets it on the door, and the moss grows well. When the spider comes out of its hole, it leaves the door wide open so that it can find its home again. The trapdoor spider likes to eat ants and worms.

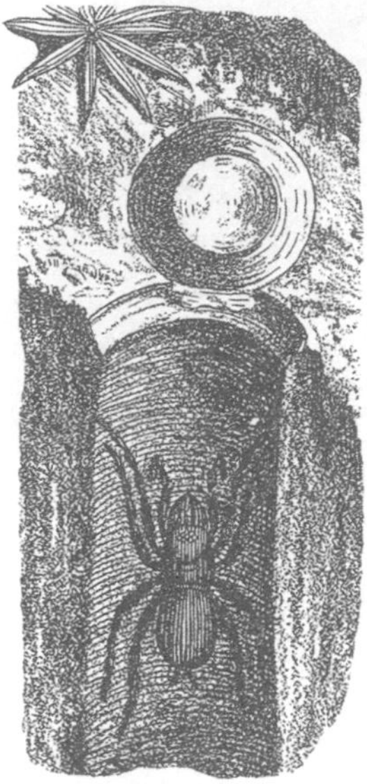

Trapdoor Spider

Once a man put a ladybug by a spider's trapdoor. The spider took the bug into its house to eat it but found that the bug's exoskeleton was too hard to bite. Then the spider took the ladybug back up and laid it out by the door. The man put a soft grub by the door, and the spider took it inside and did not bring it back. It ate the grub and was very happy.

There are other kinds of unusual spiders, too. One kind of spider makes a nest in the shape of a pear. Another kind makes a tent of leaves. It ties the leaves down with silk; then it lives in the tent and keeps its eggs there. Still another kind of spider ties a little house in the shape of a ball to stems of grass. Now and then, certain kinds of spiders eat other spiders, but not always.

The **mason spider** is another interesting spider. It is just like the mason wasp and mason bee. Do you know what a man who is a mason does? He builds with bricks and **mortar**. The mason spider, however, makes its nest of clay. It takes the clay in small bits and builds a clay house that looks like a mug; its house is six inches long. The mason spider lines it with thick silk. The door is like a box lid that has a hinge.

If you could find the odd **tower spider** and sit down to watch it build its home or catch its food, I think you would be fascinated for a whole day—or for many days. The tower spider builds over its hole a neat tower two or three inches high; then it sits on top of the tower to look for food.

Mrs. Tower Spider has as many as fifty baby spiders at once. They sit on her back for four or five weeks, until they molt two or three times. Her babies seem to get along with each other very well; they do not

Tower Spider

like to fight with each other. When Mrs. Tower Spider gets a fly or bug for her little ones to eat, first she crushes it; then the baby spiders come and suck the "juice" as she holds the food for them.

Review

1. What kind of creature is a spider?
2. How are spiders different from insects?
3. What can a spider make?
4. How does the spider spin a web?
5. Tell me about the spider's eyes.
6. How does a spider tend its young ones?
7. What does a spider eat?
8. What good things can you say about the spider?

The Spider Web

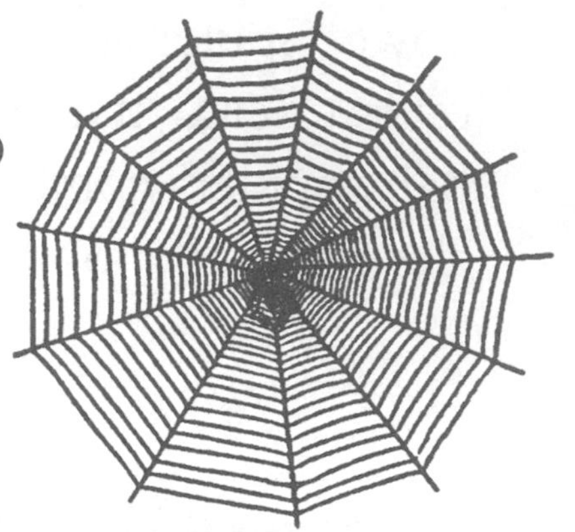

Whenever I see
On bush or tree
A great big spider-web,
I say with a shout,
"Little fly, look out!
That web seems so pretty and white,
But a spider hides there and is ready to bite."

So if any one here
Loves to sin or rebel,
I say to him now
With my very best bow,
Take care not to sin against God.
For there hides in each sin a wicked old spider,
And it fills him with joy
To catch man or boy,
And weave all about him with terrible might
The meshes of a sinful life—that hurt the soul!"

Chapter Five
All About Shellfish

Out of Harm's Way

By this time, I am sure you think that all these small bugs, flies, spiders, and crabs must soon be dead. You have learned how the cold kills them. You have heard how they kill each other. You know that men and birds and beasts kill them, too. How can any live? What is there to protect these poor creatures?

The two main things that protect them are their shape and their color. Why? How can this be? Let us see how this is done. On the sand by the sea, a crab lives mostly out in the air; it is gray in color. It has fine red spots like sand.

The crab's exoskeleton looks so much like sand that, if it lies flat and still, you can scarcely see it. The crab that lives on the mud along the seaside is the same color as the mud—black-green. Birds cannot see it very well because it looks so much like the mud that it lies on.

The bees, in brown, black, and gold, look like parts of the flowers on which they alight. One small bee that lives in trees is green, like a new leaf.

Leaf-Cutter Bee

The spiders that live in the woods are about the same color as a dead leaf. Some of them, as they lie in their webs, fold up their legs and look like a dead leaf. One spider puts a row of dead leaves and moss all along its web. It lies on this row, and looks like part of it. Birds cannot see it, as it lies in this way.

God is very wise because He protects many of His creatures in a special way. When a creature can hide by becoming like the plants or ground around where it lives, it is called **camouflage**. God made many creatures in this way to protect them from their enemies. Birds and beasts that live in snow lands are often white, as the polar bear and the eider duck. Snakes that live on trees, or on the ground, are often green or brown; they look like leaves or tree branches or **soil**. Little lizards on walls are gray like stone. In wooded areas, they often are the color of a dead twig. These lizards can fold up, or stretch out, and look like twigs, leaves, or balls of grass or hay.

Polar or Great White Bear

All this will keep them from being seen by animals that would kill them.

Some of God's creatures have hard exoskeletons to protect them. Others move fast! They dart and run and jump, quick as a flash of light. That helps them to get out of the way. God also made the crab with its eyes set on pegs. It can turn them every way to see what is nearby. Likewise, the insect and the arachnid have many eyes that help them see in all directions at once. Their eyes help them see their enemies before their enemies see them.

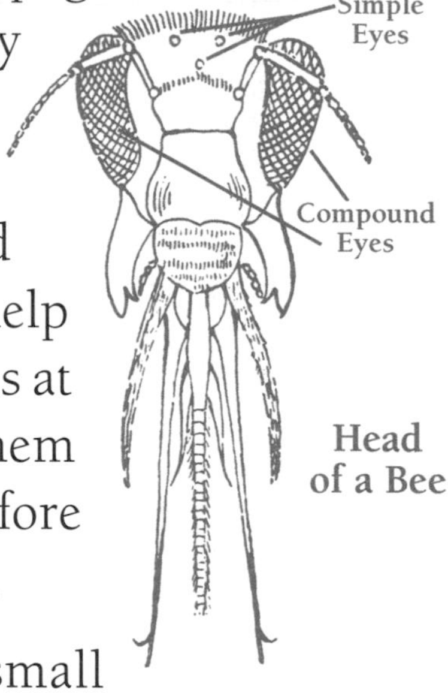

Head of a Bee

God protects these small creatures in another way. He created them to have many, many babies. There are so many small creatures that are born each year, that they cannot all be killed. For example, one crab will lay more eggs than fifty hens. One spider has more baby spiders than you can count. One bee has more new bees in the hive each year than there are people in a large city. In a wasp's big nest, there are as many wasps as there are leaves on a great tree. While many of these creatures die each day, many are left to live. This shows us that the wise Creator God planned everything in the world to work well.

Shellfish

I think most of you have heard the song, "Rock-a-bye Baby on the Treetop." What babies live on treetops? You may say that bird, wasp, bee, and spider babies do; but do you know that there are small "cradles" that rock all day long on the sea? On the waves, the cradles of many **shellfish** rock up and down. They are soft animals that live in hard shells; but they are not true fish.

True fish are creatures that live in the water and have a backbone. The backbone of a

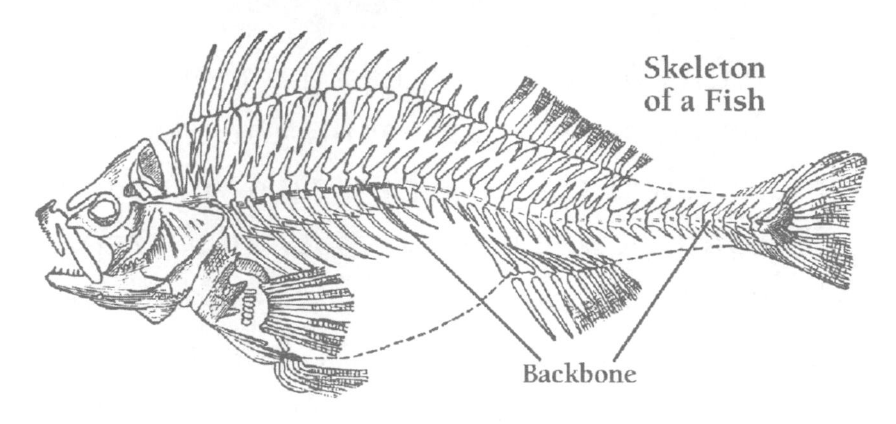

fish is very much like your backbone. All fish can swim. Most of them have fins and scales. Many of them have long, slim, smooth bodies, that help them glide easily through the water. You may see fish in the ponds, lakes, or brooks near your home. Perhaps you have eaten them for dinner. If you live in the city, you could go to an aquarium or a fish market to look at them.

In some other book I may tell you a little about true fish, but in this book I shall now tell you a little about shellfish. This is not a very good name for them, but we will use it because you will hear it from many people and will often see it used in books. The right name for these shellfish is **mollusk**, which means "soft-bodied." That suits them very well, for they all have soft bodies. They are soft because they have no bones. In the water, there are many mollusks that have no shells to cover them, such as the **squid**.

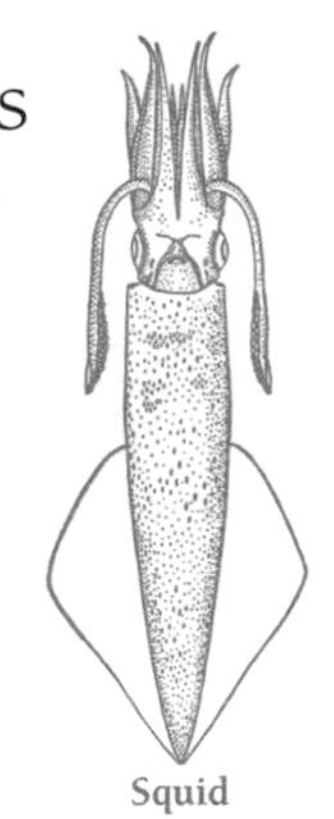
Squid

The mollusks that live in shells are mostly round or wedge-shaped. Their shells serve as "houses" to live in, as "ships" to sail in, as "coats" to cover with, and as "bones" to keep their soft bodies in shape. The shells of these soft creatures come in many forms. Some are all in one piece, like a twist or curl. Some have two parts, like the covers of a book. These two parts are held by a hinge. Other shells are made in many pieces, or scales. There are three kinds, or orders, of shellfish. The first kind of shellfish has a head on its foot; the second kind has a head, as the snail has; and the third kind, or order, has no head! Well, is that not strange to have no head at all?

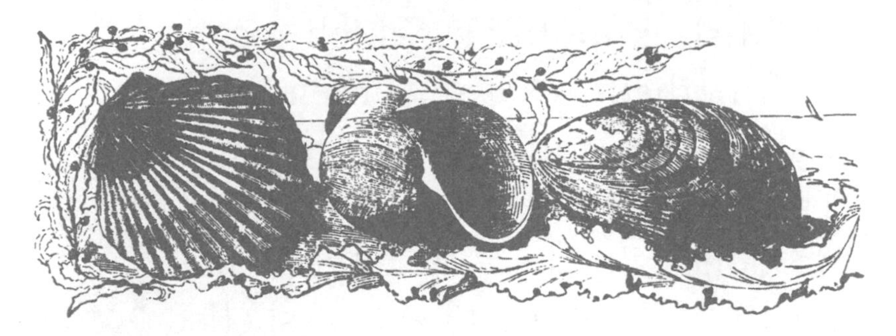

Let us learn first about the shellfish with a head and a foot. There are many kinds of shellfish of this order. They differ in size, color, shape, and way of life. If you learn about one of them, you will have an idea about all the rest of the mollusks. You know that a hermit crab steals a shell in which to live. It is often a long shell that is in the shape of a curl. Shellfish with heads live in that sort of shell, which is very hard and thick. Why is that? Since these creatures are soft and have no bones, they could not live if they did not have hard shells. Crabs, fish, and other sea creatures would eat them at once. The waves would also kill them.

The Story of Mr. Conch

Let us see how a shellfish is made. The **conch** is one of the largest you will find. Mr. Conch's soft body is tough and runs to a point. This point winds its way deep inside his shell and takes a firm hold. This way, Mr. Conch will not drop out. On one side of his body, he has a hook like a thumb, which pulls him back into his shell when he wishes to hide. The front end of Mr. Conch is wide and thick; here we find his mouth. Near his mouth he has two feelers, like insects have, to touch things. Where the feelers join his head, he has two eyes. His foot is flat and is as big as all the rest of his body. It is just the size of the open part of his shell. Why is that? The shoe on his foot is hard as a bone. When he draws back into his shell, that shoe

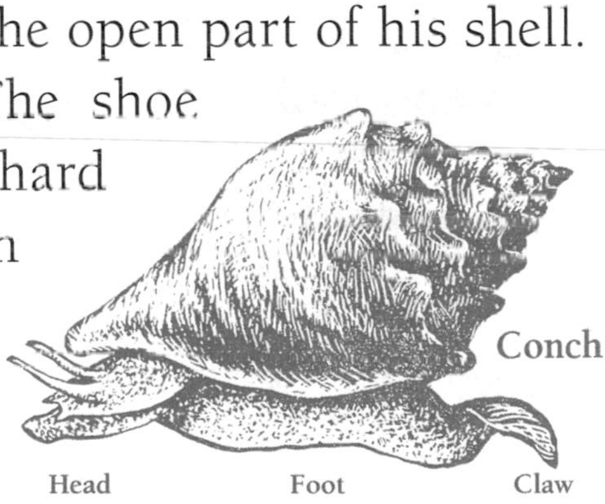

Conch

Head Foot Claw

becomes his door. It fits tight. It shuts him safe in his shell.

Mr. Conch does not like to live on dry land. He likes deep water, where he has some sand and rock. When the wind blows and the sea is very rough, Mr. Conch digs his stout foot into the sand near a stone and holds on. Then he does not drift onto the shore. If he is cast on the shore, he will die. Mr. Conch cannot live out of water. Mrs. Conch, however, likes some soft sand to make a bed for her babies. Is this not a strange "cradle"?

What does Mr. Conch like to eat? He eats other mollusks, or shellfish. He especially likes to eat oysters. How does he get them? First he goes off to the oyster beds and looks for nice young oysters. He

picks one up with his foot. He uses his foot for a hand as well as for a door. He can spread his foot out very wide. It is very, very strong. When he has the oyster in his grip, he closes his foot around it, as you would shut your hand tight. That breaks up the shell of the oyster. Then Mr. Conch easily sucks up the oyster. The men who own **oyster beds**, however, do not like him because he eats many of their oysters.

Mr. Conch lives a great many years. No one can hurt him in his hard house. His shell is the shape of a large pear. It has a little point at the top and a long end like a stem. The stem end has a groove in it. His shell turns or twists three or four times around. On the outside, the shell looks sand-colored or pale yellow; it may have dark stripes on it. On the inside, the shell is very smooth and shiny, and the color is a beautiful, bright red, pink, or yellow. It is a very pretty shell.

What is the conch good for? Fish and crabs like to eat the conch's eggs and their young ones. In some places, people like to eat the conchs themselves. Others use their shells to make beautiful buttons, fancy pins, and jewelry. The Indians used to make money from the pink part of their shells.

Baby Conchs

Now we must learn more about that string of eggs that Mrs. Conch left on the sand. First it is like a thread with knots tied close together. Then it quickly grows to be a yard long. The knots grow into little cases, or pockets. They are set close to each other. At the two ends of the string,

the cases are small, but after three or four small ones, the others are the size and shape of big lima beans.

Once I was out on the beach with my nephew Jeremy, and we found a string of this kind. It had been cast up by the waves. It was of a pale straw color and in the shape of a long curl.

Jeremy said, “It is seaweed.”

“No,” said I.

Then he said, “It must be some kind of a bean or seed.”

I said, “No, Jeremy, it is a string of conch eggs.”

Let us look at it more closely. Each case, or pocket, is flat and has a rim. The rim has lines in it. In the front edge is a small, round spot, where the case is very thin. This is the door of the case. The sides of the case are very tough. Let us cut one case open. It is full of white gum, or jelly. I see in it specks like grains of sand.

Here is one more string, far up on the sand. This one is dry, hard, and light. The little thin spots are open holes now. The cases are quite empty.

Here is one more string. This, too, is light and dry, but the holes in front are not open. Shake it. Does it rattle? Yes. What will happen if we cut a case open? Why, each case is full of tiny shells! Each shell is as small as a grain of rice! See how thin and white these shells are.

Now in these strings, you have the whole story. First, the tiny string that Mrs. Conch left on the sand grows to be a big string with large cases like these. The small specks in it become shells, and the jelly is used as food for the baby conchs while in the case. There are many, many shells in each case. They

grow and grow and eat up all the jelly. They are true shellfish, only very small. Now they must get out of their cases. They see the thin skins over the small, round holes in their cases. They know for sure that these are their doors. They eat off the thin skins and go into the sea.

Mrs. Conch lays her strings of eggs from March to May. She lays a great many of them. In each egg case, the baby shells rock up and down, not on a tree but on the sea. The dry string, still full of shells, is one in which the shells are all dead. It was cast on shore when the little shellfish were too young to come out. That made them all die. These little things have a hard time trying to grow up; but if they can live until they are a good size, they will have a thick shell. Then they will be out of harm's way and will live a long time.

Conch Shell

How does a conch grow? Does it pull off its shell when it is too tight, as a crab does? No, a conch wears a baglike "coat." It is by this "coat" that it grows. How is that possible? Its "coat" is fine and thin. It is part of the conch's body and folds all over it. This fine "coat" takes lime out of sea water, and the lime builds more shell. As the conch needs more room, it spreads out its "coat" over the edge of the shell and builds a new piece of shell with it. You can see the little rims where the coat built each new piece. The color and the waved lines on the shell are made by its "coat." The conch does not need to change his house; he just builds on more room as he needs it.

About Mr. Drill

Here is a small shellfish, or mollusk. It looks like Mr. Conch but is not so large. It is quite small; and its real size is not much larger than it is in this picture. It

is called a **drill**. Its color is dark brown, and its shell has ridges on it. The body of the drill is dark green. It has a long tail to twist round in its shell. The drill does not live in a place by itself, but a whole **host** of them live together.

The strangest thing about the drill is its "tongue," which gives the drill its name. It is like a little, soft ribbon that can move in any direction; it can even roll up or push out. Did you ever see a man use a drill? With it, he can cut a hole in a piece of wood, iron, or stone. The "tongue" of this mollusk is like a drill. How is its "tongue" made? Three rows of teeth are set in this fine ribbon. There are many teeth in each row. The teeth are fine and as hard as the point of a pin. We could not see them if we did not use a **magnifying glass**. With this fine "tongue," the drill can cut or saw a hole in a thick shell. The drill is very greedy. He eats many kinds of shellfish. He likes to eat the oyster best of all.

Oyster Drill

How does the drill get its food? It cannot break the shell of an oyster as the conch can. No, the great Creator has given the drill its own special way of working. With its tough foot, the drill holds fast to the shell of the oyster. It picks out the thin, smooth spot called the "eye" of the shell. Then it goes to work to file a hole, which takes a long time. Some say it will take two days, because it is a lot of work. It keeps a firm hold and saws away. At last, a hole is made clear through the shell. It is small, smooth, and even; no man could make a neater hole. Then it puts a long tube—which is on the end of its "coat"—into the hole. With this tube, it sucks out the poor oyster until it is all gone.

The Story of a Battle

When the drill gets on the back of an oyster, what can the oyster do? Nothing. The poor oyster cannot help himself. Do you think the oyster hears the drill's file on his shell, hour after hour? Yes. Does the oyster know the drill will get in and kill it? Perhaps it does, but all that it can do is to keep still and wait.

The oyster is not the only kind of mollusk that the drill eats. When the drill goes after the poor shellfish that have no heads, it eats them very easily. They cannot help themselves. They do not know how to get away from Mr. Drill. The shellfish that have no heads live in shells made of two parts, like the covers of a book. The two parts are held to each other by a hinge. It

is a bad thing, it seems, to have no head. Without a head, who can take care of himself?

Let us see Mr. Drill try to fight with a shellfish that has a head. Now he has met his match! He goes to the top of the shell. He takes hold and begins to file, file, file. The mollusk inside hears him. "Oh, are you there, Mr. Drill?" Then what does the shellfish do? Why, it draws its body out of the way and builds up a nice little wall! Then, when Mr. Drill gets his hole made, he puts in his "tongue" but finds no food—only a hard wall. Then Mr. Drill moves along and picks out another good place to make a hole.

Once more he goes to work—file, file, file. "Oh, here you are, Mr. Drill!" Once more, the shellfish with a head pulls his body out of the way and makes a new wall. Again Mr. Drill sticks his tongue in and finds no food. Sometimes he gets tired of the battle and goes off. Now and then, Mr. Drill finds a spot where there is no room for a wall. Then he makes his hole and sucks out the creature.

You will find many shells on the beach that have pinholes made by Mr. Drill; but you will also find other shells, like the thick clam shell, full of holes like a **strainer**. These holes were not made by Mr. Drill, however. How then, did the clam shell get so many holes? Shells are made of two different things. One is **lime**, which is hard like stone; and the other is like a dry "glue," which is not so hard. Shells with so many holes are old clam shells that no longer have the "glue" part in them. The "glue" was drilled out by a **sponge**, which is another kind of sea creature. Only the lime part, which is like a strainer, is left. Shells with only the lime part left will

Sponge

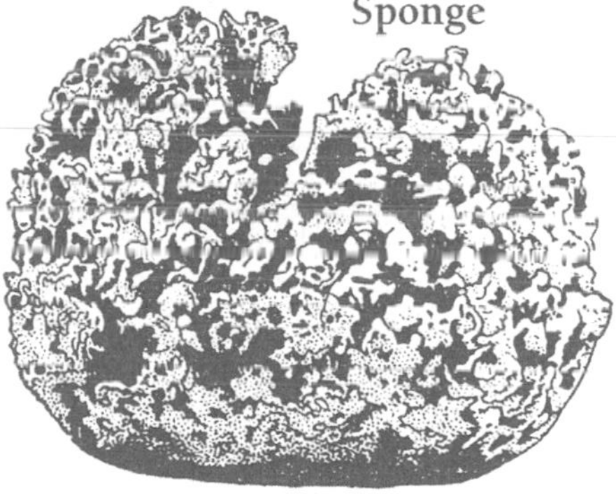

break and crack like glass. If they have too little lime, they will bend.

Even though Mr. Drill has a head, he is not as wise as he seems to be. Sometimes, he sits down and makes a hole in an old dead shell that no longer has a shellfish living in it. Now and then, he makes a hole in an old shell that turned into stone long ago. He may spend two days on a shell like this! Did you know that shells, bones, and plants sometimes turn into stone? Some day, you will learn about this amazing fact of God's creation.

How Do Shellfish Eat?

Do all shellfish feed on other shellfish? Oh, no. Some of them live by catching small bits of food—small as grains of sand—from the water. Others live on seaweed. These shellfish have long, slim "tongues" that are somewhat like a drill. These "tongues" are like small straps on which tiny "teeth" are set—three or more in a row, like the points of pins. As the "teeth" wear out from work on the tough seaweed, more grow.

A shellfish walks along on its one big foot. First, one side of the foot spreads out, and then the other. That pulls it along. It seems like very slow work, but that is all it has to do; it slowly moves about to find food. It may take it all day, but it does not seem to mind. A shellfish has no house to build and no clothes to make. It only creeps along to find a good bed of seaweed. Then it puts out its fine, filelike tongue and cuts off flakes of seaweed to eat. It never gets tired of this kind of food.

Another kind of mollusk is the limpet. It sits on a rock and has a shell like a cap;

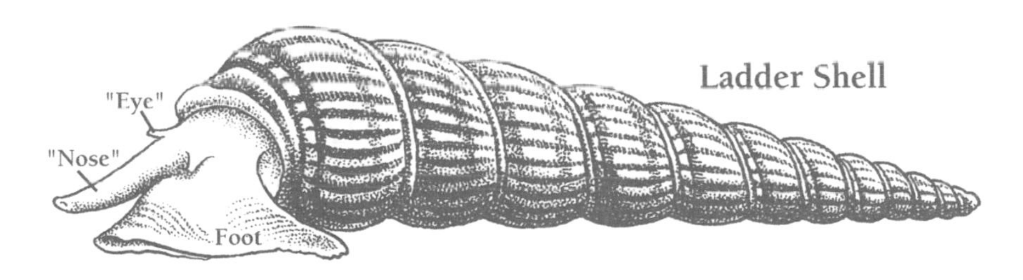

it also has a head, foot, and tongue, which is like a drill or file. It can walk along the floor of the sea and climb up the rocks. The limpet has its own rock and its own hole in the rock. It goes back to its rock when it has had all that it wants to eat.

Tortoise-shell Limpet

Keyhole Limpet

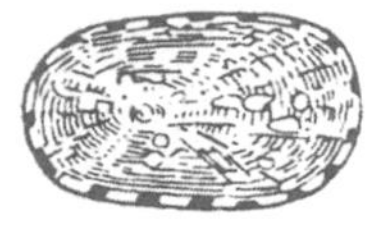

Top View

Side View

There is one nice, little shellfish, about as big as a pea. It lives in the seaweed that grows on rocks. It is brown, red, green, black, or dark yellow. This shellfish can live in the damp weeds in the hours when the tide is out and has left the rocks dry. It likes to eat seaweed. This shellfish has two tiny, black eyes and two little feelers. It also has a little snout like a small pig. At the end of this snout is its little mouth. Its small, dark foot has a dent in it. It puts out its tiny, filelike tongue and laps it out and in, as a dog does when it drinks water.

This shellfish's sharp "teeth" cut off little scales of seaweed to eat. If you take ten or more of these little shellfish in your hand, each tiny creature will draw in its little foot. As these little creatures hide in this way, you may hear a small squeak if you put your ear close enough.

The next time you are by the sea, try to learn something new about God's creation. The great Creator has filled the world of the sea with all kinds of interesting sea life—just like He has filled the world of the land. Take time to thank and praise Him for all His wonderful works.

Review

1. What is a shellfish? What are the three kinds, or orders, of shellfish?
2. What kind of shell do the shellfish with a head and a foot live in? Why do they need to wear these hard shells?
3. Do conchs change their shells? How, then, do they grow? Why are not more blown ashore?
4. What do conchs eat? How do they kill and eat other shellfish?
5. Do mollusks lay eggs?
6. What are shellfish good for?
7. What did the Indians make out of the shells?
8. Tell me how Mr. Drill does battle.
9. Of what are shells made?
10. How is Mr. Drill's tongue made?

Chapter Six
All About Worms

Mr. Worm and His Family

One day I saw a boy making a hole in the ground. When he dug out a worm, I asked the boy, "What can you tell me about worms?"

The boy said, "Worms are long, soft things, alike at both ends. If you cut one in two, each end goes off and makes a whole new worm. They have no heads, no feet, no feelings, and are no good but for fish bait." The boy thought he knew all about worms, but really he knew very little about them. Nearly all that he had told me was wrong.

Worms belong to the great class of ringed, or **segmented**, creatures called **annelids**. These creatures have bodies made in rings, or **segments**. If we take a closer look at our humble friend, the earthworm, we will see that it is a long, round, soft, dark, slimy thing. You might say, "It is alike at both ends"; but is it? Let us see.

Mr. Worm's body is made from one hundred to two hundred segments. These segments are smaller toward the two ends of his body—one end is his head and the other his tail. Each ring has eight tiny hooks, or **bristles**, too small for you to see. The worm uses these hooks to move along and dig his way in the ground.

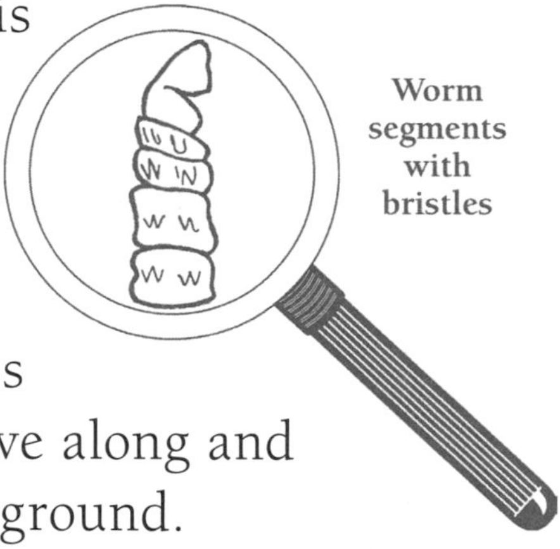

Worm segments with bristles

Mr. Worm can hold so hard to his den, or hole, that you have to work to pull him out. Have you seen Mr. Robin brace his feet and tug with all his might when he pulls out a worm? The worm is holding fast by his hooks. You see, the hooks are like Mr. Worm's "feet."

Let us now look for Mr. Worm's head. You have five senses; you can hear, see, feel, smell, taste. The earthworm can also feel and taste. Some think Mr. Worm can smell some things, but he cannot see or hear. So what makes him come up to "look" around, if he cannot hear or see? He is feeling rainwater or dew filling his hole. He cannot breathe when water fills his hole; he may even drown. If he has no eyes, ears, or nose, why do we say Mr. Worm has a head? We say he has a head because he has a mouth and a tiny brain. His mouth has two lips. The upper lip is

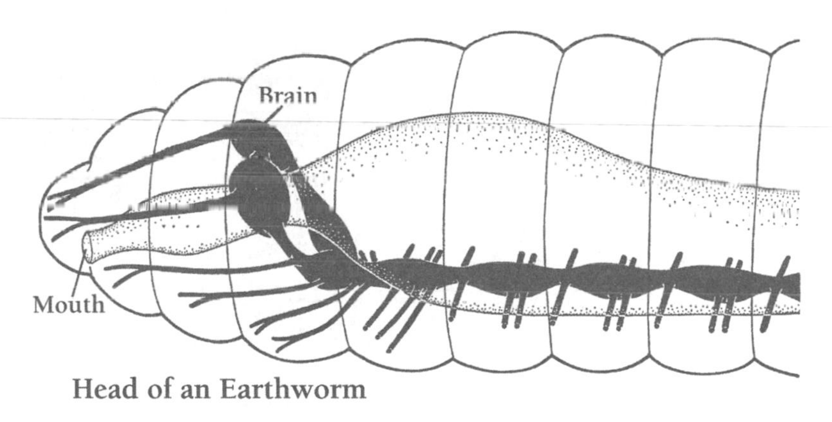

Head of an Earthworm

larger than the lower one. Mr. Worm has no teeth, though. In the back of his head, not far from his mouth, is his brain, or **nerve** center.

The worm is the only segmented animal that has red blood. Mr. Worm is dark-colored because his body is full of the earth that he swallows. If you keep him out of the earth for a while, his skin will get pale and clear. Then you can see his red blood run in two long **veins**. He needs fresh air to keep this red blood pure. He dies very soon if he is shut up in a closed box or case. If you look closely, you can see Mr. Worm's ten hearts! He has five hearts on each side of his body.

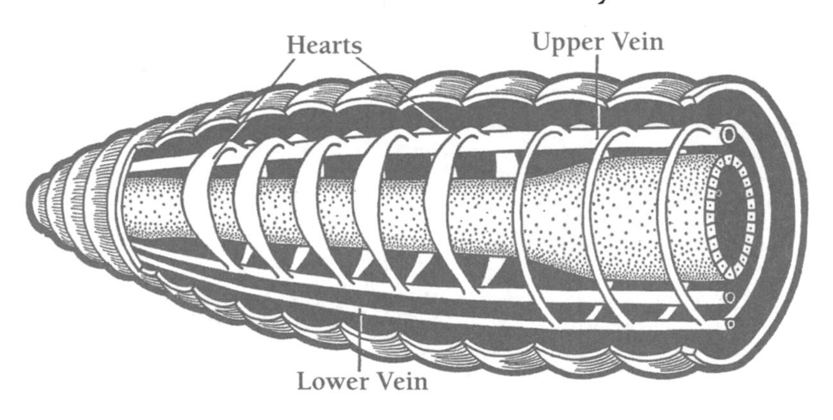

Mr. Earthworm at Home

I told you the earthworm has two veins. One runs down his back; the other runs along the underside of his body. There are tiny holes, like pin pricks, in his body. These holes let the air reach his blood and keep it red and pure.

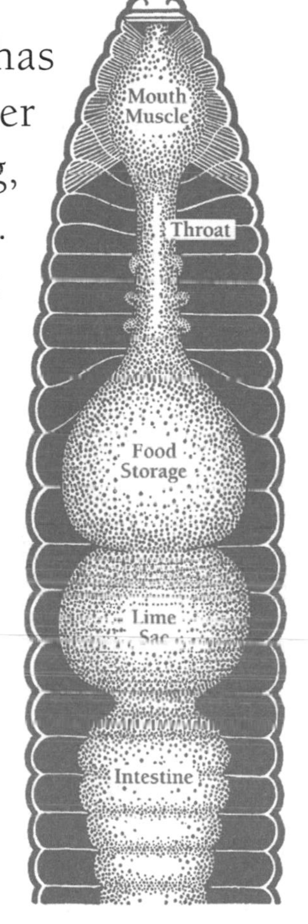

In his body, Mr. Worm has something that no other creature has. He has a bag, or sac, which holds **lime**. This helps him to **digest** his food. God did not give Mr. Worm any teeth with which to grind his food. How does he chew, then? Inside his body, he has small bits of stone. These are as small as grains of sand. They are used instead of teeth to grind his food. The little sac of lime helps to grind or change Mr. Worm's food so he can use the food he swallows. The soft body of Mr. Worm stretches like rubber. It holds a great deal of food.

Now you see that Mr. Worm is not alike at both ends. One end has his head, "stomach," parts that serve for a brain, and ten hearts. The hooks begin at the fourth ring behind his head. If you see Mr. Worm when he lifts his head, you will see his mouth. The other end—his tail—has very strong hooks with which to hold fast to his cell. This tail is also his **trowel**, or scoop—a tool that Mr. Worm uses to build up the **soil**.

Ah! Now I have told you a great thing, a wonderful thing. Is it true that the "feeble, useless" worm helps to build up the soil? Where is that boy who knew so much about worms?

Before you learn how the worm helps to build up the soil, let us go back to what the boy said. He stated, "If you cut the worm in two, each end will go off and become a whole worm." This is not true of the worm. When the worm is cut in two, both ends will not live. Since there are hooks and rings on each end, the ends can move off. If the front part of the earthworm is safe, the cut can close up, and the worm can still live. Then a new tail can grow, just like Mr. Crab's claw or Mr. Spider's leg. The back part, however, cannot live and grow. It cannot get a new mouth or heart, so it cannot eat food or have any blood. It soon dries up and dies.

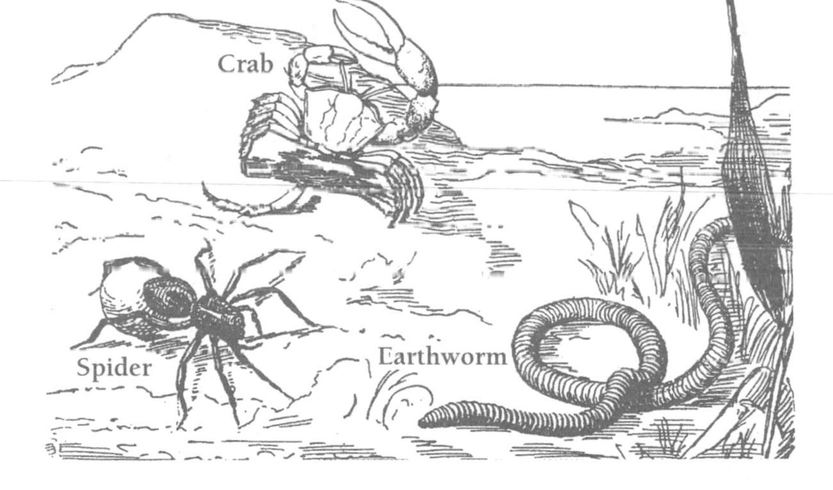

The boy also told me that the worm "had no feelings," but a worm can feel. The sense of touch is the best sense it has. If you put your finger on its body, you will see it move and **shrink**. As you come near his house, Mr. Worm may crawl up, poke his head out of his hole, and wag it back and forth. He does this because he feels the ground shake as you walk.

The worm cannot see. Creatures that live underground have little use for eyes. If the worm moves from the light and hides from it, it is because it feels the warmth of the light on its skin. When the sun comes out, the worm goes down in its hole where it is cool and **moist**.

What does Mr. Worm eat? Some tell you that he eats dirt. It is true that he fills his body full of soil. He does this to carry it to the top of the ground. Mr. Crab has claws and legs to bend into the shape of a basket, but poor Mr. Worm has no arms, legs, or claws, so he must make a "basket" of himself. Suppose you should be sent for fruit, and turn yourself into a basket in that way! Your mother would be very surprised because she would not wish you to become like a worm.

It is true that worms may find a little food in the soil that they swallow, but the chief food of worms is dead leaves and stems of plants. They do not care for fresh leaves or stems that are still alive. Worms also like meat—raw or cooked. They will even eat the bodies of dead worms. Best of all, worms like rotten onions and cabbage. They simply pinch off a tiny bit of food and swallow it.

Worms also need plenty of water, so they find a damp place to live. They will soon die, however, if they are put into water. Worms will choke because they cannot breathe in the water. When the worm gets food and water into its mouth, the rings of its body begin to move out and in. They look as if they were opening and shutting. By this motion they press their food and drink down into the body.

When the worm wants to move, it also moves its body. It stretches out its body to its full length; then it takes hold of the soil with its hooks. Next it draws up its body, and so moves on. This is a wavelike motion. Watch it, and you will see that it travels up and down like a wave.

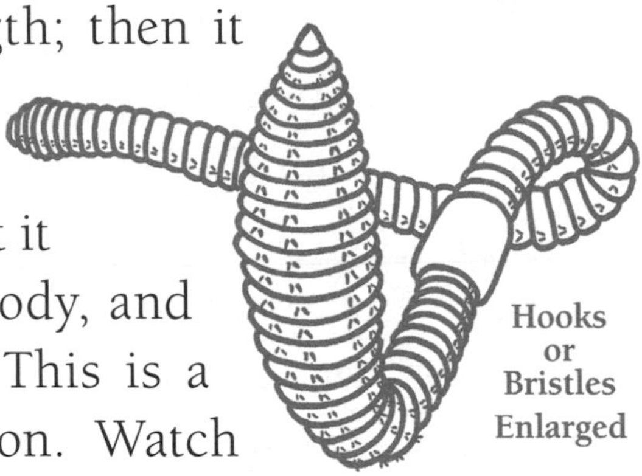

Hooks or Bristles Enlarged

If you wish to find worms to study, you must look for them early in the morning or late at night. The best time to find them is when the earth is moist with dew or when it is raining; but they **avoid** the heat of the sun. Worms hurry to the surface of the soil to enjoy the falling rain and so they can breathe. When there is a long, dry time, the worms go down deeper and deeper into the soil; you will not be able to find them when you dig for them. They need to stay down where the earth is moist, soft, and cool.

Mr. Worm at Work

Worms are found in all parts of the world. I have told you that they help to build up the soil and make it fit for plants to live. In turn, these plants help man to live. Man cannot live without the food that plants produce, and the plants cannot make food without the soil. The worms help to prepare the soil for plants to produce man's food. It is wonderful that humble, dirty worms can be such a help to man! Man is the highest work of God's creation, and worms are nearly the lowest; yet God created the worms to help man live.

Now let us see how this is done. The worms live under the ground and make long, winding "halls," or tunnels, some inches below the top soil. These little tunnels help to keep the earth loose, so that the fine roots of the plants can grow well in the soil. These tunnels also help the air to move more easily through the soil. By their constant motion below the surface, worms till the soil below, like rakes, spades, or plows till the soil above. All this is part of God's great plan for His creation. Stop and praise Him for His wonderful works.

You may hear people say that the worms have eaten up the seed sown, or the worms have bitten off the roots of the plants. Some even say that the worms cut the vines below the soil, but do not think that earthworms would do such a thing. Not at all! They never behave so badly. When people speak of "worms" doing this kind of harm, they mean the grubs, or larvae, of certain insects, such as the **owlet moth** and **pyralid moth**. Their grubs—called cutworms and webworms—eat living plant roots; but true worms only like to eat dead leaves and stems. They want their food made soft by decay.

Now we come to the chief work of true worms. When they make their "halls" and houses, they fill their long bodies with soil. Some say it is their food, but they fill their bodies with soil just to get it out of their way. If they get any food from the dirt, it is not much. They turn themselves into "baskets" to carry the dirt out of their houses.

The worms work, work, work all the time, swallowing soil and carrying it to the surface of the ground. There they pile it in heaps. Each piece is the shape of a small worm. The soil takes this shape as the worms press the soil out of their long, soft bodies. Early in the day, and also after a rain, you can find these little heaps of soil over all the garden paths. There are so many worms busy all the time that each year they bring up tons of earth. This shows you the power that such small, weak creatures have. In India, there are some earthworms that make heaps six inches high!

Worms make the soil fine and loose by pinching it off with their mouths

and bringing it up to the surface of the ground—then they go back for more. People used to say, "Oh, no, no! It cannot be true that little, soft worms could cover a great field, some inches deep, with fresh soil"; but it has been shown to be quite true. Fields once stony and hard have become rich and fine. Things now grow where once they could hardly grow. Ashes and gravel, that used to cover the ground, are now found two or three inches below the surface of the ground. All this is done by the busy earthworms. That is why I said that you could call the tail end of the worm the tool that helps it build up the soil.

Worms at work underground have caused great walls and pavements to sink. They also have helped to bury ruins and old cities, keeping them safely hidden until they are found later. We are glad to learn about the ancient world from these ruins that worms helped to hide. Worms also help make the soil rich with the dead leaves and stems that they drag into their holes for food or protection. These plant parts decay in the soil and make it better for plants to grow. When worms die, their bodies also help to make the soil more fertile.

Worms That Live by the Sea

On the seashore you will find two or three other kinds of worms. These are called "tubeworms" because the shape of their houses, which they build, look like tubes. Some of them are called "swimming worms." They are similar to another family of creatures that look like worms but have many feet. These creatures are called **centipedes** or **millipedes**. Do you know what their names mean?

Centipede

"Centi" means **hundred**, "milli" means **thousand**, and "pede" means feet, so their names means "hundred feet" and "thousand feet."

Now let us look at the seaside worms. Here we find some worms that have eyes. We also find some that have little hard teeth that are set in a ring inside their mouths. There are others that have small, fine **plumes** that look like the large, beautiful feathers of certain birds. These humble worms gleam like a rainbow. New parts can also grow on these worms just like they do on earthworms—only better. Some say that they can even get a new head if the old one is lost. Some of these worms can **bore** into very hard things, such as wood or stone. Some of them shine like a fire; you might even call them "glowworms."

If you dig in the sand along the sea, you will find worms that are black, brown, green, red, or orange. They dig through the sand and mud and move very fast, but it is not yet known how these worms bore into stone and wood. Perhaps it is by means of some kind of **acid** in their mouths. Perhaps they have a file, like Mr. Drill has. If you look along the seashore, you will find the tubelike homes of these sea worms. They are like little shellfish because they make their shell-like homes larger by adding a little bit to the end of their houses as they grow. Most of these tubelike homes are small, but some are very large. A gentleman once told me he saw one with a **bore**, or hole, as large as his arm.

These sea worms are food for many fish and other creatures. You know that nearly all fish like to eat worms and that they are used for bait. At least the boy who did not know much about worms knew they made good bait. He would have been amazed if I had told him that some large worms are used for food by men in different parts of the world.

Mr. Worm at Home

Baby worms are just like parent worms, but they are smaller and do not have as many rings. As they grow, they get more rings; a ring is added when the last ring of the body divides into two. In the right kind of soil, the tiny baby worms are born in little hard skin bags, or **sacs**, which keep them from harm until they are strong enough to take care of themselves. When they are old enough, these young worms immediately begin to dig houses, carry out the soil, make heaps of soil, and find food. God made them to know at once all that the older worms do; God gave them these skills at birth, so they do not need to be taught.

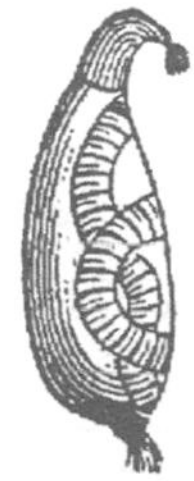

Egg of an Earthworm

Worm baby coming out of its egg

Mr. Worm's home is like a row of long "halls," or tunnels, that are not deep underground. These tunnels are lined with a kind of glue from Mr. Worm's body. This glue makes the walls firm. If the weather is very cold, or very dry, he digs down deeper. Mr. Worm does not like the cold or **drought**. He enjoys warm weather the best. He also likes water and wet soil. When the winter comes, Mr. Worm plugs up the door of his house. This is done by dragging the stem of a plant into his doorway; this plant stem fits perfectly and becomes the door of his house.

The worms carry into their homes leaves and stalks to eat. They bring out and throw away things that they do not like. Worms show much sense in the way in which they carry things in and out of their holes. If a stem will not go in, the worm will turn it over and try to fit it in some other way. Worms usually come out of their holes at night or in wet weather. If they go far from their house, they cannot find their way back; then they make a new hole. Each worm lives alone.

Often in the evening or early morning, or during rain, you will see worms near their houses. You may find them with just their heads out of their doors. Early in the day or after a rain, you will also see their heaps of soil because this is one of the few times that worms dare to come out. Sun and heat dry worms up very fast, and soon they will die.

Birds know all the ways of these worms. Watch Mr. Robin, for example, as he searches for his food at sunrise, after sunset, or while it rains. Look! His keen

eyes see a worm at its door! In goes Mr. Robin's sharp bill, and then he grabs the worm and pulls hard because he is hungry and wants his breakfast. The worm, however, holds fast by its hooks, or bristles. Then Mr. Robin braces his feet and tail and tugs even harder. Out pops the poor worm, and Mr. Robin eats it for breakfast. Mr. Robin shows great skill in the way he pulls the worm out of the hole. He does not break off even one little segment of the worm's soft body. No boy could get the earthworm out in that way.

Some say that worms lie by their doors at sunrise for warmth; I do not think that is so. I think what they like is the fresh dew. Worms love dampness, but they fear the cold and could die from heat. In less than one day, worms will die in dry air, but certain kinds of worms can live for weeks deep down in the water. Most important, worms need an even, moist warmth to live. Their homes must not be hot or cold or dry.

Sea worms make the prettiest houses. On shells, stone, wood, or wound alone in a lump, you will find their tubes. On the outside, these hard, shell-like tubes are white; but on the inside, they are pink or blue. These tubes curve and twist about in the same path that the sea worms travel as they build them. Some tubes are very pretty.

There is a soft kind of tube made of sand and bits of shell, stone, and weed. The sand and weed are held together by a kind of glue. Worms make this glue in their mouths. Some of these tubes are very clear and white. You can see the lines where the worms went as they built them, ring by ring. Some of these tubes are so small you can just run a fine needle into them. Others are as large as a straw, and still others are as large as a fine, fat earthworm.

Now you see how much can be learned, even about such a small, humble thing as a worm. Think how much such a weak creature can do! There is much more to be found out about worms, which I hope you will be glad to learn for yourselves by carefully studying God's creation.

Giant Australian Earthworms

Review

1. To what family of creatures does the earthworm belong? What did you learn about this ringed creature?

2. How do the rings in a worm's body increase in number?

3. What kind of food do worms eat? How do they chew their food? Do worms harm crops or grass when they eat?

4. Is a worm "alike at both ends"? What is each end like?

5. If a worm is cut in two, will both parts live? If so, how?

6. How does a worm make its hole? Why is it so hard to pull a worm out of its hole?

7. How do worms help to build the soil? For what other reasons are worms useful?

8. What kind of weather do worms like best? What do worms do in very hot, dry weather?

9. How does a worm close up the door of its hole? Why does the worm do this?
10. When can you find worms outside their holes?
11. What do you know about sea worms?

Epilogue

Things Are Not Always What They Seem

"What beautiful light that lamp gives," said Mr. Moth as he stood on the window ledge.

"Yes, it does," said Mrs. Bee, who flew with great difficulty toward Mr. Moth. "But you would be better off staying away from the lamp. It is not safe at all."

"Surely there can be no danger there," said Mr. Moth. "The flame looks so cheerful and bright."

"Yes, but the nice-looking light burns those who go too close," said Mrs. Bee. "I am in pain right now because I went too close to the light and it burned my wing."

"I really think you must be mistaken," answered Mr. Moth. "I do not see how that pretty light can harm anything. Perhaps you were just too careless. I shall fly to it and see for myself."

"You can choose to not listen to my words of warning," buzzed Mrs. Bee. "But remember, things are not always what they seem."

"All right," responded Mr. Moth with an impatient voice. But a short time later, he flew straight toward the flame and soon fell to the floor, badly burned and near death.

As Mrs. Bee flew past Mr. Moth, she shook her head and said, "Foolish Mr. Moth, you can't say that nobody warned you. The bright light of temptation and pride can often blind those who will not listen to good advice."

Many boys and girls who have trouble staying away from foolish and harmful things could learn from this story. Too often, children become blinded by the bright lights of sinful pride and go after foolish things that are harmful to their bodies and souls. Remember, my friends, that the true Light of the world is Jesus Christ. If you want to be safe and happy forever, be sure to walk in the light of God's Word—the Bible. Do not trust in your own wisdom, for in a sinful world things are not always what they seem!

The Boy That Never Sees

God help the boy that never sees
The butterflies, the birds, the bees,
Nor hears the music of the breeze
When zephyrs soft are blowing;

Who cannot in sweet comfort lie
Where clover blooms are thick and high,
And hear the gentle murmur nigh
Of brooklets softly flowing.

God help the boy who does not know
Where all the woodland berries grow;
Who never sees the forest's glow
When leaves are red and yellow.

Whose childish feet can never stray
Where nature doth her charms display—
For such a helpless boy, I say,
God help the little fellow.